A YEAR
WITHOUT
A NAME

A YEAR WITHOUT A NAME

CYRUS GRACE DUNHAM

Little, Brown and Company
New York Boston London

Little, Brown and Company
Hachette Book Group
1290 Avenue of the Americas, New York, NY 10104
littlebrown.com

First Edition: October 2019

Little, Brown and Company is a division of Hachette Book Group, Inc. The Little, Brown name and logo are trademarks of Hachette Book Group, Inc.

The publisher is not responsible for websites (or their content) that are not owned by the publisher.

The Hachette Speakers Bureau provides a wide range of authors for speaking events. To find out more, go to hachettespeakersbureau.com or call (866) 376-6591.

ISBN 978-0-316-44496-5
LCCN 2019937210

10 9 8 7 6 5 4 3 2 1

LSC-C

Printed in the United States of America

A YEAR
WITHOUT
A NAME

PROLOGUE

I COULD TRY to tell a story that ends with resolution, but the only way to succeed would be to lie. If I lied, I would be whole at the end of the story. Wholeness would be possible. I might superimpose alienation onto every moment of my life leading up to self-acceptance, as if denial and repression are not so powerful that they create their own truths. Then, upon narrative completion, I would correct the condition of never having felt at home in my body. I would find personhood, once and for all, hospitable and harmonious. I would be an individual, an adult, a man.

But I have, at many moments, believed I was a woman. And in that belief, which did not leave any space for doubt,

I *was* a woman. What is womanhood, anyway, beyond a belief that constitutes itself?

I will never have been born a man. I do not propose this as a universal truth. Some other people I love feel differently. I may pass as a man someday, but I will know in my gut that I had to convince myself I was allowed to have that passing, that I sacrificed for that passing, that passing feels like a betrayal of everyone who ever loved me as a woman, for being a woman. And maybe I will always wonder if that passing is just a trick, a lie. The trick might be a deeper truth than the girl, the woman, or the man. The trick itself might be who I am.

My name was Grace. The first thing I remember is a purple morning glory out a window. The second thing I remember is slugs on the wall of a shed. My mom had me when she was forty-two. She tried hard to have me. She had a green piece of paper with all the names my parents almost named me. My mom wanted to name me Esther and my dad wanted to name me Kay. They agreed on Grace. They only put one boy name on the list, Cyrus, which sounded like Osiris, the ancient Egyptian god of rebirth.

My mom's ancestors were Jewish and my dad's ancestors were Puritans who I imagined wore only black and lived in wooden houses where there was nothing soft to sit on. Puritans had names like Hope, Mercy, and Patience, which were similar to my name. They were ideas, not things you could touch. This distinction became important to me: Grace was an abstract noun; bird was a concrete noun.

My mom went to a psychic when she was having trouble getting pregnant with me. The psychic told her there was a baby boy waiting to enter their family. The psychic said the baby boy had chosen them because he had things he wanted to teach them. My mom told me that story often. It made my face get hot. I wondered if the baby boy was me.

My mom is a photographer and my dad is a painter. My dad and I drew together every night. When we finished a drawing, we each signed it on the bottom right corner. His signature started with the letter C, which looked like a mouth opening up and spitting out the rest of the letters. I couldn't spell so I copied his signature, except I started mine with a G, which I wrote like a C with a tongue. I liked to draw Gs walking across the page with their tongues getting smaller and smaller until they became Cs. I liked imagining myself as my dad when he was a little boy. I looked at old pictures of him standing on the beach and pretended I was inside his body.

My sister is six years older than me. She had wavy blond hair and she liked the things I hated, like makeup, dresses, and jewelry. She kept a pile of dolls and I kept a box of superheroes. She gave me her old dolls and I used my grandpa's old tools to saw their arms and legs off, unscrew their heads, and drill holes in their torsos. I did the same things with my superheroes, then put the different limbs back together to make creatures that were part doll and part superhero.

My sister liked to paint my face with eye shadow, blush, and lipstick, dress me up, and take photos of me. She put red glitter on my eyelids. The glitter was in the shape of lips, stars, and hearts. I parted my lips and held my breath while she snapped through Kodak disposable cameras my parents had bought for her at the drugstore.

We went to the Metropolitan Museum of Art every Saturday morning. I liked the arms and armor section, with its rows of metal men and horses. I liked how the armor was big and heavy, but there were little drawings of flowers scratched into the surface. I pictured myself running through a forest, with armor for skin.

When we drove through other parts of the city, I hoped for red lights so that our car would stop and I could see into the windows on the lower floors of apartment buildings. Later, I fantasized about the rooms I'd seen and imagined I was part of another family, but a son instead of a daughter. It scared me that I only got to be one person the whole time I was alive. Even if I had been reincarnated, I couldn't remember who else I'd been.

At school, I was only friends with boys. Kids made fun of the boys who only played with girls, and those boys' parents were embarrassed by them. My parents were proud of me because I was a special, tough kind of girl.

I had short hair I slicked back in the bathroom with water, and a heavy leather jacket my mom bought for me at a thrift store. I sat with my legs spread wide and picked the scabs on my knees until they bled. At home I stood in front of the mirror with my shirt off and my arms crossed, lifting my chin up like men in magazines. For a while I told my sister and my parents that I wanted to be called Jimmy, which was the nickname of the actor James Dean and of my mom's best friend, whom I never met because before I was born he died of AIDS. No one agreed to call me Jimmy, but I still liked to say it out loud to myself in the mirror. "Hi, my name is Jimmy," I would say, then repeat it three more times, to make it even. "Hi, my name is Jimmy. Hi, my name is Jimmy. Hi, my name is Jimmy."

During the summer, we left the city and went to a house across from a lake, which was connected to another lake. The lakes were called Twin Lakes. I loved the summer because we left the windows open. I could hear crickets at night and birds in the morning. When I could hear the outside through the window I didn't feel like I was trapped or like I was going to die, even though I knew everything would die eventually, including the sun. My dad had told me that someday the sun was going to explode and get so big that it would swallow up the earth. Then it would shrink and turn red. After that the sun would get cold and dark, then disappear. But by then everything I knew and loved would already have been destroyed.

In Twin Lakes there were older girls who lived up the road and invited me over. They had me pretend to be their husband or boyfriend, which meant I took my shirt off, kept my shorts on, and lay on top of them moving my hips back and forth while they made noises. I held my hand between my legs like a penis. This made a tingling feeling start in the bottom of my back and move out through the rest of my body. A girl in the neighborhood had a teenage brother with short hair he dyed bleach blond and a red convertible. He sped home late at night to the end of the dirt road they lived on. He wore tank tops and a seashell necklace. When I was alone in the yard behind the house I rolled my sleeves up and walked back and forth pretending to be him.

I went to a camp near Twin Lakes where one of the counselors had long, wavy hair and big boobs. I stayed close to her, asking her how she felt about her parents, her friends, and boys. She said I was a really good listener and that she could talk to me in a way that was different from how she talked to other people. I loved listening to her. It made me feel important. She let me stay with her while the other kids did activities. We made up reasons, like that I was sick, or that she needed my help with something. Once while it was raining out she let me lie on her chest in an empty tarp tent. She whispered in my ear how special I was, four times. "You're *so* special," she said. Special. Special. Special. Special.

1

I NOTICED ZOYA right away. She was standing in a group of friends, outside a half-demolished art deco hotel in Pune, the city where she grew up, smoking under a veranda. She wore trousers and a high-collared shirt and smoked with her arms crossed in front of her, on guard. She had big eyes, somewhere between probing and alarmed. I zeroed in on her.

Almost immediately, I was ready to devote myself to her. Devotion is the closest thing I've known to a stable gender, insofar as our gender is a set of rules we either accept or make for ourselves.

We met on January 26, 2017, six days after Trump's

inauguration speech and two days before my twenty-fifth birthday. I'd just driven from Mumbai to Pune, the second city of Maharashtra, with my friends Akhil and Prab, with whom I was traveling in India. Akhil and Prab were both there visiting relatives. They were also both nonbinary and transfeminine, and for this reason, the trip was divided into two chapters: familial first, gender transgressive second. I followed along for both. Whenever my bodily claustrophobia grows unbearable, I seek new lovers, new locations, new friends. So be it. Novelty is the longest-lasting short-term coping system I know of.

Zoya and her friends stood under the hotel's former carport. Half of the hotel's exterior walls were missing. You could see into the rooms, like a dollhouse. The hotel had been turned into an art space, where Akhil would be performing that night. Ruins of luxury repurposed for culture.

Throughout the afternoon, I took inventory of everything Zoya said: She was born in Pune but hadn't lived there for nearly a decade. She had gone to school in England. She was a writer. So far, no indication as to whether or not she would be attracted to me, which was the primary information I was searching for.

In the early evening, I took a seat in the back row to watch Akhil do a version of the performance I'd seen them do many times now, both on this trip and before. They have an uncanny ability to stand in front of a room and, with a quick scan, assess the alienations and resentments of the crowd. In between recitations of poems about the tangled pain of gender and colonialism, they offer impromptu sermons. As they preached toward different demographics represented in the audience, I catalogued my own supposed identities. Woman: I'd already failed at that. Were I to become a man one day: I'd calcify into an apathetic voyeur, so protected by privilege as to be incapable of feeling. White person: my subjectivity was irrevocably distorted by my violent inheritance. This calculus made failure feel inevitable, resistance an impossibility.

At some point during their performance, Akhil paused and summoned me to the front of the room to read a few short poems. Zoya was in the front row. I averted my gaze. It was humiliating to follow Akhil onstage.

As a teenage girl, I'd stood behind the podium in debate tournaments and wielded language to assert my intellectual superiority. I spoke in neatly constructed paragraphs with clear arguments. One of the privileges of white girlhood was feeling entitled to prove that I was the best. I was taught to believe that winning would correct for centuries of oppression. Girlhood loomed larger than my own power.

Now, with my girlhood dissolved and no clear alternative in place, I felt the least entitled to take up space I ever had. The specter of sexism no longer fueled me. I wasn't technically a man, but if I ever successfully embodied masculinity, I'd stay standing in the corner watching, my hands crossed behind my back, where men should be. My friends and lovers would know not to call me forward.

* * *

When, around the age of five, I began to recognize myself in words, I was afraid of the words that described me being found out. The words were always in my mouth. They felt like part of me. My parents and their friends cherished me for being a little girl. I knew I was a pervert. I was tricking them.

When I figured out how to spell the words I held in my mouth, I wrote them over and over until they filled up the page. "I'm gay I'm gay I'm gay I'm gay. I'm gay I'm gay I'm gay I'm gay. I'm sick I'm sick I'm sick I'm sick. I'm gross I'm gross I'm gross I'm gross. I'm a boy I'm a boy I'm a boy I'm a boy." Then I ripped the pages up and flushed them down the toilet.

The first person I devoted myself to after my mother was a girl in my class named Anna who wore a pink bow in her hair every day. She had long brown hair. She liked to draw, or play with dolls, or sit in the corner of the playground and wait for people to come to her. She didn't like to get dirty or be rough. Boys tried to wrestle with her, and it was my job to protect her. We sat near each other on the rug while our teachers taught lessons, and we found ways to touch each other when no one was watching. We also kissed when we could. At home, my sister found a piece of green paper with a heart and Anna's name written on it. I had copied the shapes from the name tag on her locker; I was still learning to spell. My sister told me it wasn't okay because we were both girls.

12

I learned the word "desire" and I knew having it meant I wasn't innocent. I saw a blond girl in a pink bikini at the public pool near my cousins' house in New Haven. I went to the locker room and threw up. In the attic bedroom at their house, I had a dream about the girl from the pool being underneath me, her arms and legs tied to the bed. I'd only seen people tied up like that in movies where women got kidnapped or held hostage. In the dream, she loved me. For days after I didn't want to talk to anyone. I couldn't stop replaying the dream.

The grown-ups around me had no idea what was happening inside my mind. But I knew what to say to make them love me. It was so easy to impress them. All I had to do was ask questions, listen closely, and ask more questions. Adults were lonely and wanted someone to talk to, even if it was a child. I taught myself how to engage in conversation while replaying my secret thoughts. The distance between the inside of my mind and the world around me grew.

The times I liked best were when I could be in my mind without anyone interrupting me. In these private moments, I could replay things that had happened to me: the girls up the road, the camp counselor who said I was special four times. Special. Special. Special. Special. I could also imagine moments that hadn't happened: kissing, holding down, and tying up girls I'd never met, in faraway places like tropical islands, or motel rooms, or the classrooms of Catholic schools. I couldn't not replay them: four, eight, twelve, or sixteen times, the numbers kept me clean.

When I fixated on a girl, I'd list and describe every inter-action we'd had: instances of physical contact; what she'd worn each day of the year; the days she'd been absent; every word she'd spoken to me. I wrote her reverent letters. They were carefully observed character studies, meditations on her insecurities, hopes, dreams, and fears. Without the courage to reveal myself, I destroyed the letters upon their completion. Writing toward someone helped me break out of my own obsessive monotony, if only briefly. I didn't need her to know. I just needed someone to reach toward.

After Akhil's show, a group of us went to a Persian restau-rant where we smoked hookah on a wooden porch. I sat down next to Zoya. When she spoke, she used uncommon words with many syllables. She chain-smoked. She said she was an alcoholic, said she was kidding, then said she was serious. She told me about a conspiracy theory that the CIA had introduced the water hyacinth to the river systems of the Indian subcontinent to intentionally desecrate native species so that communities would be dependent on Amer-ican exports. She looked at me earnestly and said, "How can you think about anything besides climate change?"

Right now, all I could think about was whether my desirability would be more enhanced by my hair falling in my face or resting tucked behind my ears.

"It's hard," I said. "To think about anything else."

When the restaurant closed, we went to a bar down the road, where drunk straight people danced to house music.

A white man put his arm around my shoulders and asked me whether I liked Indian women. Zoya observed the inter-action, visibly disgusted. Hatred of men, particularly on the part of a woman whose affirmation I longed for, made me that much more determined to cling to femaleness.

The bar closed, and Zoya took a group of us to her parents' house—a marble-floored flat in a tall, modernist building on the edge of town. Her mother greeted us at the door in a nightgown, trailed by two fluffy orange cats. We all sat on the balcony. I listened to other people's conversations and continued to drink, unsure of what else to do.

More people arrived, and I snuck away to snoop around her family's apartment. I looked at the books on her bookshelf—classics of feminist autofiction; photographic and cinematic theory; tomes of Indian history I wasn't familiar with. I looked for family photos in the living room. I looked for any evidence to help me shape myself into someone she'd desire.

I brought Akhil with me to the bathroom, where I forced them to analyze the likelihood of Zoya's interest.

"How do I know if she likes people like me?"

"Why, because you're white?"

I assessed myself in the mirror. I worried I looked too much like a boy. From another angle, I worried I looked too much like a girl. I knew I would tilt myself in whichever direction Zoya preferred.

I was binding my breasts, but their curve was still visible under the fabric of my shirt, a mound of flesh pressed under elastic fabric. The immediate urge was to cave in, hunch over, round my shoulders forward so that the breasts were protected, if not entirely hidden. Any insinuation of my breasts undermined my capacity to believe I was desirable.

When I was thirteen I found swelling in my chest, under my nipples, while I was in the shower. When I pressed the skin, it hurt. I screamed, ran out of the bathroom still wet, and told my mom there was something wrong with me, that I was growing tumors. She said it was just the beginning of my breasts growing. "Like flowers," she said. "They're called breast buds." I had dreams about cutting them out with a knife, like pits from a peach, and throwing them into the dirt so they could grow somewhere else. She took me to the doctor for a checkup and they had me take my shirt off and lie on my back on the exam table. The doctor kneaded the skin on my chest and pressed around the swells. She told me puberty was starting.

That week in the shower I picked up my mother's pink razor and shaved all the hair off my legs, arms, and knuckles. I shaved the fuzz off my face, too. And when I got out of the shower I pulled the razor down between my eyebrows, over the hairs above the bridge of my nose that my dad told me were "severe" and "beautiful." I didn't use soap, so by nighttime I had red bumps all over my arms and legs. I tried to hide the rash from my parents by wearing long-sleeved shirts and pants, but I wasn't good at pretending and they asked me why I wouldn't put on my pajamas. My mom said that if I wanted to shave, she'd teach me. My dad was upset. He told me women didn't have to get rid of their body hair. But I needed all the parts of me to be smooth in order to be okay with what I was growing into.

From that point on I had a semi-addictive relationship to mirrors. I left class as often as I could just to look at myself. When other girls came in, I pretended I'd been washing my hands. I couldn't walk by windows without following my reflection, a doll moving along next to me. It seemed like if I didn't check my appearance all the time, as often as I could, something terrible would happen. People would figure out that I was disgusting and that this condition could not be fixed. Other girls started making fun of me for being vain. I forced myself to look at the ground, sat through class, and pushed down the compulsion to make sure I hadn't accidentally revealed something. It felt like being a girl could slip away from me at any moment, if I didn't check four, eight, twelve times. If I failed at being a girl, I'd reveal the truth: that I was inherently perverted.

The bigger my breasts got, the more I wanted my body to shrink. That only seemed possible through deprivation. The game was to get so hungry that I was dizzy and then stay in the dizziness, to try to focus in class and ride the subway home and do my homework all while being nauseous from hunger, which was its own type of energy. I was tired all the time. It was hard to open doors or pick up my backpack. I found huge bruises on my legs, purple,

17

pink, and blue, until they turned green and yellow, and I didn't know what they came from. I was disappearing and that was what I wanted.

I was examining the fruit bowl in the dark kitchen when Zoya entered behind me.

"I was looking for fruit."

"I was looking for you."

She cut up some pineapple, which we ate together, and poured me a glass of vodka without ice. I stood closer to her. Someone else entered the kitchen. I was drunk now, and from then on I trailed her.

We ended up on her bed with a group of people I didn't know. I woke up disoriented, my head on her chest, to the sound of her whispering, "They're asleep."

Though I'd been passively occupying the singular gender-neutral "they" for two years, I still couldn't summon the certainty to ask for it. When it was used in relation to me, I accepted it. I accepted "she" as well, though it registered as a sharp reminder that my attempts at something other than femininity were failing. Asking to be regarded in a specific way required the courage to claim an identity. I preferred to observe what people wanted me to be and politely follow suit.

Zoya referred to my gender indeterminately without it having been discussed. "They're asleep." Two words, and she summoned me into existence, became the keeper of my unrealized self.

Akhil shook me from my resting place on Zoya's chest

and told me it was time to go. The sun was coming up; we had a train to catch in two hours.

"I don't want you to leave," she said.

"Come with us."

I brought her with us in a taxi and we kissed sitting on the ledge behind the half-demolished hotel. Mid-kiss, I already wondered how I could see her again. Her friend interrupted us, pulling up abruptly on his scooter. He grabbed Zoya and told her to get on so he could take her home. She hopped on without saying goodbye.

Akhil, Prab, and I were in Mumbai on my twenty-fifth birthday, which fell on the same day as the city's pride march. We sat in traffic for an hour trying to get there, stopping at a blockade and running to catch up with the crowd. The event was rife with familiar symbols—rainbow flags, equal-sign banners, Lady Gaga impersonators. There were also unfamiliar symbols: impersonators of Bollywood icons, gender-nonconforming people communicating the specifics of their identity through aesthetic and cultural codes I couldn't understand. Akhil and Prab explained certain things to me—the origin of a specific textile, the caste connotation of an earring placement—and left me living in ignorance of others. That which I wasn't meant to understand, I suppose. I liked being prevented from knowing. Peering in from the outside thrilled me. Call this the white gaze, the unrealized, already-failed-at-male gaze. Or call it longing. Either way, I'd felt it since I could remember.

Zoya was supposed to join us that night. I bought a six-pack on the way home from the parade and drank two beers to try to slow down my pulse. It was a hot night. Akhil and I walked around the corner to a barbershop, looking for a barber willing to trim their mane, a mop that fell in front of their eyes in tumbling ringlets. I sat behind them, witness to the male drag required for them to be shaven.

I was sure Zoya wouldn't come until she arrived. When I saw her stepping out of a taxi outside the barbershop, I strode out to greet her. Practice made it possible for me to walk slowly, calmly, resisting the inclination to run toward her. The alcohol made it easier to reach out and pull her toward me, kissing her on the cheek with the confidence I had hoped for.

We had sex for the first time that night. She braided her fingers around the back of my neck. We lay in the dark talking, her head on my chest, and then had sex again. The second time she whispered in my ear that she wanted to be overwhelmed entirely, that she hoped this was okay. I was relieved to decenter my own body, rather than having to summon the vulnerability it takes to be inside it. Always more in tune with my partner's desires than my own—a false binary, perhaps, when you prefer someone else's pleasure to yours—I've grown accustomed to leaving my body when lovers want to touch me, attempting to anchor myself through the satisfaction in their faces. If I direct all of myself toward my lover's pleasure, I can ignore my breasts, my hips, the flesh covering my muscles and bones. Why focus on my body when I can only experience it as excess?

After I made Zoya come, she said, "Thank you," like I'd done my job.

The next week, she met us in Delhi and took me as her date to a brunch at the home of some prominent arts patron, a postmodern mansion overcrowded with expressionist paintings and marble sculptures. This home belonged to the sort of family that had built my parents' careers and, as such, sustained the comforts of my upbringing. I'd been accompanying my parents to events of this nature since I was a little girl, and I knew how to stay in character: polite and grateful, curious and engaged, self-assured and humble. The only difference now was that I hoped to cut the character with masculinity. To channel composure, I pictured an unassuming, handsome man with his hands in his pockets, leaning against a wall, unafraid of having no one to talk to, immersed in observation.

At this point, she knew virtually nothing about me. I'd overheard her tell someone my name, but she'd gotten the second part wrong. I took this as proof that she liked me neither because of nor despite my affiliations. I was hesitant to correct her, though I worried my omission verged on manipulation. In being unknown to her, I could relax. All she knew was what I'd given her, what she'd gleaned. And, if her language was any indication, she saw me as neither male nor female. Intoxicatingly, she appeared to believe in my ambiguity.

In the backyard, waiters served Bloody Marys and trays of hors d'oeuvres to European curators and wealthy

Indian art collectors. I drank two Bloody Marys in quick succession, smoking a cigarette next to a table covered in a pink tablecloth, while Zoya made her way around the party chatting. Periodically, we stared at each other across the lawn, but I tried to stay still and grounded in my body, my gestures. I knew how to look around the room, curious but without demands. The goal was for my masculinity to function like armor, without making me into a man, per se. She'd made her disdain for men clear. I added it to my own disdain—read: emulsified envy and fear.

Zoya returned to my table and asked how I was doing. I told her I was having a ball, people-watching, enjoying the pleasures of my own company.

"You're very beautiful, you know," I said, after a pause. She looked away and took a drag of her cigarette. Not a thank-you or even eye contact as acknowledgment; she changed the subject to the land reclamation of Mumbai at the hands of the British Empire. I feared I'd recast myself as a groveling male, biologically programmed to be overwhelmed by her good looks, too dumbstruck to notice how profoundly she didn't care. I wanted to clarify and explain myself. Instead, I said nothing, afraid to break character.

That afternoon, she took me to an art fair—aisles of objects, people crafting identities through studied consumption. This, too, was a familiar scene. Nearly every weekend of my childhood, my parents took my sister and me to brightly lit white rooms where people crowded around art and drank wine out of plastic cups. I remember getting a bad feeling in my chest when grown-ups looked around the room, worried about whom to talk to next. The more they drank, the more they talked. Women took me to the bathroom with them while they reapplied their lipstick, or let me come into the stall with them while they peed. Afterward they'd tell my parents how special I was, while I pretended not to listen.

Now I followed Zoya dutifully as she took me on a tour of the work she found interesting. I asked thoughtful questions. Really, I just wanted to know if my statement earlier that day—you're beautiful—had closed my access to her completely. A few times, I grazed her back with my hand, hoping for a gesture in return. She was focused on the art. I grew more anxious, more frustrated with my own anxiety.

Later on she took me to a party at a modernist embassy. Security personnel flanked the entrance. Inside, young people bounced up and down to EDM. I wandered away from Zoya, convinced that I needed to perform disinterest to stay desired. Eventually she found me and brought me to a marble terrace for a cigarette, where we chatted with a handsome man who appeared to be in his early thirties. They had a rapport; she brought him into our conversation, asking him what he thought about my statements, asking me what I thought about his. He spoke slowly and thoughtfully, gesturing with his hands. He wore glasses, and his thick hair kept falling in his eyes in the middle of his sentences. He pushed the hair back with one hand, smoked with the other. He passed Zoya the cigarette periodically, as if he knew when she wanted it without her saying so. My jealousy pulled at me, sensing her admiration of him and suspicious of their familiarity with each other. Always torn between treating my jealousy like paranoia and treating it like intuition, I tried to suppress the discomfort in the back of my neck and listen, engage in conversation politely and normally. Did he find her beautiful? How could he not? And did she find him handsome? How could she not? I reminded myself that I was unfamiliar to her—a well-spoken and attractive outlier who brought dynamic ideas and different reference points (didn't I?), who offered aspects of masculinity while still constituting queerness. This was the type of script I'd learned to recite to myself when jealousy threatened to crumble my sense of self-worth. A behavioral therapist had once taught me to use rational analysis to undermine the voice inside my head. Proof against and proof for: as if two columns of facts could provide me with the information I need to feel desirable. Column A: she didn't touch me; she hasn't looked at me in five minutes; I stare at her more than she stares at me. Column B: she said she loved having sex with me; she did touch my back one time earlier; we just met; I'm crazy.

I wanted her to stop talking to this man. I wanted her to kiss me. I wanted her to tell me she wanted me. I wanted not to need those things. I wanted to be someone who wasn't already cycling through the same old obsessions, grasping for proof that someone I'd slept with twice cared about me. I wanted to be this luscious-haired, distinguished man. I wanted to punch this luscious-haired, distinguished man in the face.

The man asked me a question, but I'd been so focused on the contours of his face, the line of his biceps and pectoral muscles under his linen shirt and the particular way that the collar revealed his sternum, that I hadn't heard what he said. My insecurity made me myopic.

I tuned back in, tried to quiet the surveyor in my mind, who intended to analyze every part of his body and compare it to every part of my own. I asked him questions about his career in academia and about contemporary politics, listening to the answers just enough to formulate the next intelligent question.

In the car on the way back to the hotel, she told me she didn't want to have sex that night. I was a deft enough performer to immediately thank her for telling me, express my gratitude that she felt comfortable being honest.

"Do you think I'm a prude?" she asked.

"Never," I said. "Of course not."

"It's just that I don't feel like I know you, yet. And I want to talk, to feel like I know you."

Then I asked her about the man. I tried to reframe my jealousy as openhearted curiosity, in the hope it would slip under her radar.

"Who was he?" I asked. "I really liked him."

"You did? Yes, he's special. He's just a friend of mine."

Her casual admiration made my face get hot and my fists tighten up.

"That's so nice," I said.

She'd rented a guest room in a neighborhood called the New Friends Colony. We tiptoed quietly to her room, to avoid waking up the guesthouse's resident managers, who had warned her against young women coming home late. We lay down on the bed next to a pile of outfits she'd been choosing from earlier. She rested her head on my chest. It calmed me down. I worked up the courage, a little tipsy, to apologize for telling her she was beautiful earlier in the day.

She told me I didn't need to apologize. I pushed her to tell me how my saying that had really made her feel.

She explained it was something she'd been told often, and it wasn't what she needed—or wanted—to hear. I tried to swallow my embarrassment and told her I wouldn't say it again.

"Okay," she said. "Don't. Tell me other things."

And then I tried to explain to her—my first attempt, I think, at stepping out from behind my laconic facade—that it was different for me. I wanted to be told I was handsome, to be longed for. I was nourished by adoration; whether or not it is a quick fix for a deep lack, it lifted me up, at least momentarily. She listened quietly and, when I'd finished, said that it was okay to need different things.

"You shouldn't be afraid of wanting me," she said. "I'll tell you if it's too much for me."

We held each other for a while and then she told me that she'd lied to me earlier, about the man.

"We had an affair," she said. "I was embarrassed, because I don't even like men. But it felt quite queer, how much he worshipped me."

I listened quietly, enraged and aroused. My character's job was to understand why she'd done what she'd done, affirm her desire, and defend her actions. It made me more attracted to her to imagine her with him. I'd never say that out loud, though; I'd never admitted to a lover that when my attraction waned, I imagined them with a man—the last one they'd loved, maybe—engulfed in pleasure, as if I had never existed, would never exist. This vision usually revived my interest.

We stayed up talking. She'd showed me the effect worship had on her, and this intensified my fixation. Now I had something to invest myself in. We stayed up until the slit of sky between the curtains turned pale blue. I wrapped myself around her. Close to sleep, she said my name like she was asking a question.

"Grace?"

The next night, the fourth we spent together, we went to a party at a villa outside the city. I'd been waiting all day to be alone with her, maybe because I wasn't getting the attention I wanted; maybe I needed a level of attention no person could conceivably give me. I feared that, at the party, I would inevitably lose her to small talk. I did, and I took the time alone as an opportunity to dance with myself and wander around staring at people. Periodically, I'd bring her a drink without interrupting, or try to look handsome and severe while she introduced me to someone.

After an hour of wandering, I pulled her into the bathroom and pressed her against the wall, reaching under her dress. I couldn't tell whether her resistance was part of the game, and my uncertainty made me tentative.

"This is too premeditated," she said. We returned to the party.

I was drunk enough not to feel completely spurned, but ashamed I hadn't known better. I felt like a little girl, too self-conscious to get anything right. And also, like a man. A boundary-crossing, despicable man.

I drank the shame off, ordering round after round for us both. We danced, together and with her friends. As much as I longed for her attention, I liked watching the ease with which she moved through the room, the seriousness with which she spoke about ideas, even in settings like this one. And when she danced, which I hadn't yet seen her do without hesitation, she threw her head back and laughed, seemingly toward no one. It turned me on to observe the details of her personhood outside me.

Too shitfaced at the end of the party to figure out how to get home, she collapsed onto a bench at the edge of the garden. Her friend got us a taxi to share with two rich girls (Zoya called them that; I wouldn't have opened myself up to the accusation of being called one, too). I spent the ride home putting all my energy into keeping down the swell of nausea rising in my chest. When we arrived at the guesthouse the gates to the building were locked. It took another thirty minutes to walk the perimeter of the compound and find a night watchman to let us in through a back gate. We stumbled back to the building, where she intermittently yelled at and shushed me, dragging me to the roof for her final cigarette of the night.

One cigarette turned into two, and soon she wanted to drink more. She had taken a bottle of something from the party. I couldn't say no.

There was messy sweetness between us again. I was learning that she saved her affection for our time alone together. She kissed my cheek, and I wrapped my arms around her body.

"Hi, Grace."

"Hi, Zoya."

"Hi, Grace."

We passed the bottle back and forth. I told her I was too drunk. She said the alcohol would help.

We went downstairs and climbed into bed. I undressed her and kept my clothes on, lying on top of her with my arms around her. In the dark she pressed her lips against my ear and asked me to overwhelm her.

This was an audition: What if I wasn't sharp enough with my language? What if I didn't walk the line between care and humiliation with enough mastery? What if I took my confrontations too far? Was I putting on a show, or trying to reflect her back so clearly that she couldn't live without me as her mirror? Did she want me to worship or degrade her? Were the two different?

I told her to say what she meant and stop hiding behind complex concepts and big words. Then I told her to drink less and stop fucking men because she was bored.

Her breathing changed and I entered the meditation of controlling another person's experience entirely.

I told her, in quick succession, not to lie, hide, evade emotion, or ever think that she could do anything without my seeing her underlying wishes and fears. I told her I knew her better than she knew herself.

She lay flat on her stomach; I fell asleep draped across her back and slept through the night.

The first night I truly slept embracing someone was also the first night I had sex. I'd slept pressed up against friends before, but never had I wrapped my body fully around someone else's. At least not since I was a little girl, nestled against my mother.

The first person I had sex with was a girl I'd been obsessed with since I was fourteen. She read alone on the steps during lunch instead of socializing. She had an older boyfriend. She was a beautiful writer. I was enamored of her combination of solitude, talent, and promiscuity.

The night after my high school graduation we had sex on top of the pink linen sheets of my parents' bed. She lay on her back and I put my mouth on her and my fingers inside her. I'd thought about these actions so many times that it seemed as if they had already happened. She didn't try to touch me, and I was relieved. Being touched never figured into my fantasies. When I imagined her she was always with a boy, handsome, kind, and subdued, until she was underneath him. I was not him, but I flickered in and out of his body, in the glow of her love.

I woke up with her sleeping in my arms, my face buried in her hair. Sex had finally happened outside of me, in the world, with someone. I was real now.

It didn't last. As soon as we were apart, I replayed the encounter until it was as immaterial as all my other fantasies. Somehow, my fixation on having sex again was much more insidious than desire in the abstract. At least, when I'd only had sex in my mind, I relied on myself for fulfillment. Dependency on another—for validation, for existence— was precarious. But there was no turning back.

Later in the summer, curled up in the dark in my adolescent bedroom, she cried when I touched her and told me she wanted to be my best friend, my sister, my daughter, that she wanted to *be* me, but that she wasn't in love with me. This was an early introduction to the multiplicity of roles wrapped up in queerness, though I didn't narrate it as such at the time. My worst fears had been confirmed: my touch was so unwanted that it brought my beloved to tears. My desire was inherently violating.

I spent the rest of the summer holding her hand and sleeping with my arms wrapped around her, adamant that the ways she needed me were enough to fulfill my own needs. In August, I went with her to a cabin in Maine with no electricity, where she spent the summers with her mother. The night we arrived on the island, we had sex on a rocky beach next to a bioluminescent bay. She was the only body I had ever been inside of (though I lied to her about this, to gain the protective armor of experience), and I couldn't summon, or even imagine, desire for anyone else.

We slept on the beach, and in the morning I leaned over to kiss her. She leaned away and said, "You want more? For me, it's like there was a bubble growing inside of me. Then it burst. Now I'm satisfied."

I did want more. I lied and said, "I understand."

If I couldn't be the boy she desired, at least I'd be the girl who understood.

I convinced Zoya not to return home when she'd planned to; instead, we went away for two days to a regal, shabby hotel in a fifteenth-century fort on the side of a mountain that she'd once heard was "romantic." She ordered a taxi to drive us there in the dark.

The drive was two hours; we stopped once at a McDonald's in the shadow of two empty, unfinished high-rise buildings, with no windows, but neon signs that read "The Paradise" and "The Escape." We kissed in a bathroom stall, and I told her that, in Maine, McDonald's serves lobster rolls; in New Mexico, sopapillas. She pulled me back to the car, where we rode in silence, clutching each other.

Our room was high up in the fort, with an arched stone

ceiling and tall wood-framed windows that opened out to balconies. We flopped onto the bed, little girls in a hotel, then dissected the particularities of the context, whom it was meant for, and how it came to be. The fort had once belonged to a king who filled its rooms with wonders and oddities.

She wrote and I read next to her; every fifteen minutes or so, she'd take a break and kiss me on the cheek. It was the first night we spent together that we didn't drink. When she was done I pulled her to bed, where we stayed until sunrise, talking. Mostly, we talked about writing—whether it mattered, why she wanted to do it. I told her I wasn't sure if I had it in me, that I couldn't write without feeling my words were an unnecessary contribution. She agreed and disagreed, which made me trust her mind.

"Falling in love makes me want to write, though." I garnered strength from indirect confession. Vulnerability without submission.

She was silent for a moment.

"Please don't turn me into a fiction," she said. "It would be a shame if you did."

What would become of us if we wrote each other into our records? What could she mean to me, over time, if her love was the narrative device that brought me into being?

We woke up late, disoriented, the sun already in the middle of the sky. I lay on the bed watching her get dressed—picking which trousers to wear, applying perfume, gathering her things. Something I'd taken comfort in since

I was a child, sitting dutifully on the bed watching my mother practice the same ritual.

She wanted to see the town, and so we walked slowly down the hill. As we made our way down the tiered levels of the fort—all of which had been turned into sitting areas, dens, lounges for the hotel guests—she talked to me about this "colonial fantasy" we were participating in, allowing ourselves to romance each other inside of. She continued the game of prodding at my involvement.

"Would you like a camel ride? Would that add to this fantasy, make your experience that much more authentic?"

It was becoming clear that she, like me, struggled with a secondary, analytical voice that prevented her from taking total pleasure in anything. Whether it was sex, a beautiful room, a quiet walk—we were in any given moment until one of us stepped outside it to qualify and undo it.

On the town's main street, a dirt road lined with vendors at the bottom of the hill, I became nauseous. Zoya sat me down on a stone step and went to find me a Coca-Cola. I watched some dogs and pigs rooting through a pile of trash, ringed by the moat of a drainage ditch, until she returned. She placed her hand on the back of my neck and held the Coke while I sipped it from a straw. She stroked my neck.

She surveyed the town's main street. "Trash in the roads," she said. "Trash in the rivers. Trash in the ocean. Trash filling up the world." She couldn't separate the apocalyptic from the romantic—the former informing the imperative for the latter.

The town smelled like jasmine and burnt plastic. I asked her if she thought it was possible for a white person to write about India, in any way at all, without reiterating tropes of orientalism, without falling into romantic exotification.

"Definitely not," she said. "But one could try."

We walked by a gated girls' school with two symmetrical painted peacocks facing each other above the entrance. A small sign on the gate read, "We shape our girls in such a way that they will have radiant faces, inquisitive intellect, strong willpower, and self-reliance in life."

"That's us," Zoya said. "We're very good girls."

She was joking, but this was exactly the type of girl I had tried to be, had been praised for being.

"I have an idea that might be silly," she said. "Should we get a photo taken?" Two doors down from the pharmacy, in a six-foot-wide storefront, a young man sat behind a computer, surrounded by color-corrected, almost fluorescent photos of babies, couples, teenage girls, and families. Each subject posed in front of a different background—a regal palace, a grassy pasture, an interior whose furniture was printed with pineapple motifs. She explained that the photographer would shoot us in front of a blank white wall, then decide for himself what background to place behind us. We would get two copies, three hundred rupees, or thirty cents, each, and the original image too, if we liked. We sat in the waiting room, finishing the Coke. She told me about the history of these photo studios, which had arrived in India in the early twentieth century. People traveled for days to see themselves captured in a photograph for the first time.

We entered the photo studio and let the photographer tell us what to do with our bodies. He gestured for me to lift my chin, for Zoya to demurely lace her fingers together at her pelvis. He placed me behind her and wrapped my left arm around her waist. I was the groom and I liked it. He flashed the bulb twice and told us to come back in thirty minutes.

When I was a kid, my mom took pictures of dolls and ventriloquist dummies. She had metal cabinets where she organized toys by color and size—plastic cowboys, plastic horses, and plastic housewives. She had every kind of food, but miniature. When there was film left on the end of a roll, she let me shoot pictures on her camera. After she got them developed, we looked at the slides together on a light box.

"You and your sister," she used to say, "are the best works of art your father and I ever made."

Zoya and I walked down the road holding hands. It was getting late, and the whole town was bathed in yellow light. Rows of teenagers were walking home from school, groups of girls holding hands. An older man shook my hand and welcomed me from America.

We passed a clothing outlet called Facebook Fashions, a banner (same font and logo as the corporation) hung between two buildings. We each took pictures of the other in front of it, and she continued to tease me. "You can tell your friends that, in India, they name stores after social media platforms. We're just that desperate to be Western."

She bought an apple at a fruit stand for a donkey at the hotel we'd seen tied to a tree. She explained that she'd have to take bites out of the apple and feed them to the donkey herself. We walked by a stand selling pale green, gray, and orange scarves, and she suggested I use them as pocket squares. I asked her to pick two for me, and she chose pale blue and pale gray crisscrossed with a grid of red lines.

At some point I asked her if she thought we looked strange to people. She replied, tersely, that nobody cared—either we were friends holding hands, or I looked like a man. We continued to negotiate this tension—between my curiosity about how we appeared in a context unfamiliar to me, and her impatience with my assumption that our behavior was any riskier here than in the spaces of my American life.

We returned to collect our photographs. We each got an envelope with two glossy pictures inside it. I'd like to be someone pictures didn't matter to, but I've always cherished photos of myself and someone I love or long for. Proof that I am, in fact, a person who loves and is loved, who fucks, who is coupled. When I see an image like this, it still feels like a miracle. Me? My arm around a woman? A beautiful woman?

The sun was setting. One side of the sky was still pink, fading into a deep, bright blue. It was almost a full moon. On the way back up the hill, we passed a big willowlike tree emanating a chorus of high-pitched calls. A peacock lifted from a branch and flew in front of the moon, landing on a telephone wire. I screamed because I didn't know peacocks could fly. She told me not to talk, and soon I could make out two, three, five more peacocks, perched throughout the tree like it was their house. I asked if they were wild, and she whispered they were probably put here, a long time ago, by the king, to make people feel royal; but now, what's the difference. I tried to talk again and she put her finger over my lips, shut me up so I wouldn't scare them off. We stood there in silence until it was too dark to see them, except for the ones on the branches closest to the orb of the moon.

I said the image reminded me of a tarot card—the peacocks crossing in front of the rising moon felt like a prescient symbol, one meant for us and us alone. I wasn't sure what the message was, but I wanted this moment to be a signal. I wanted proof I was in the right place. I wanted proof that I was falling in love with a person, not grasping for myself.

There was hardly anyone on the return flight. Each passenger had a whole row. Foggy after two glasses of red wine, I lay splayed out under the prepackaged blue blankets and watched *Deepwater Horizon*, a big-budget movie about the 2010 oil spill in the Gulf of Mexico. Mark Wahlberg played the protagonist; a pale, beefy family man who had contempt for BP executives and an intuitive relationship to the black sludge he and the other offshore drill operators sucked from the bottom of the ocean. Halfway into the film the rig explodes. For the remainder of the movie, a group of white men, with the exception of one black man and one Latina woman, caked in blood and petroleum, navigate the flaming rig; one character is burned alive, another crushed to death, others catapulted into the ocean. Ultimately, only Mark Wahlberg's character and the woman survive.

The film was a parable: men destroyed by the extractive industry for which they are the foot soldiers. Except for Mark Wahlberg, the hero. During the lowest depressive dips of my closeted high school experience, I googled Mark Wahlberg multiple times daily. Young Mark Wahlberg. Young Mark Wahlberg in a wifebeater. Shirtless Mark Wahlberg. Mark Wahlberg girlfriend. I ran my eyes over the notches of his six-pack, the way his briefs hugged his hips without skin pushing out over the edges, the ratio of length difference between the sides of his dark brown hair and the top.

In the middle of the second leg of the trip, I dreamed I was in a small plane with an unfamiliar man, flying low in the dark above water, toward uninhabited mountains faintly visible in the distance. We dropped. I hoped our momentum would propel us over the mountains to a landing strip. But we couldn't make it. I came to consciousness in frigid water, in near pitch black, tangled in seaweed. I intuited that the man was dead, facedown in the water. I was alone, no light or sign of company in my worldview.

I woke up to Amelia Earhart's voice, a fast, indiscernible

whisper. She'd haunted my mind since I was eight or nine, when I found a book about her in the library of my new school. When she was a little girl in Kansas, she made long lists of the most successful men in industries like sports, politics, Hollywood, and business. I kept lists too. I wrote down descriptions of all the types of facial hair I'd seen in one day, or of the most handsome men I saw on the subway. I had a little table where I drew and made things, and I hid the lists there, underneath other stacks of paper. At night I went through the lists in my mind, imagining my dad in the outfits of men I'd catalogued, then imagining myself in them too.

In one of the books about Amelia Earhart, I read about an old woman in Florida who claimed she'd heard Amelia's voice calling for help on her transistor radio when she was a little girl, her SOS sent across the world as a misdirected radio wave. I told my dad I couldn't sleep because I heard Amelia's voice calling out to me, speaking over my thoughts, like she had out of the radio. Amelia was there inside my head. During the day her voice was on top of my voice, so fast and afraid that I couldn't understand myself. When I looked down at my body, I wondered if I was just a doll or an action figure. What did it mean to be alive? Was I real? Would I just disappear in the night, like Amelia had? If people were looking for me, how would I know? I would be utterly alone, until I was nothing.

The closer we got to LAX, and the farther I got from Zoya, the more my neuroses set in. I could hardly eat

the complimentary dinner because of my obsessive calcula-
tions about its nutritional content and its sourcing. What
chemical pigments had they added to make the flesh of
the farmed salmon appear pink? In what ocean was this
particular salmon's floating net cage? How many millions
of other salmon lived alongside it in its feedlot? How many
people had been underpaid to handle it? How long was it
frozen before being reheated in saffron dill cream sauce?

Political analysis becomes its own kind of pathology. One
learns to locate violence in even the most intimate and banal
moments. Sex: a rehearsal or a failed rejection of power
differentials. Drinking: a market-driven addiction we use
to momentarily forget we're in the midst of the apocalypse.
The top of the mountain near my house in Northeast LA:
where I can see which homes belong to people who believe
they deserve to keep their lawns green with water piped in
from Colorado. I've used deconstruction to distance myself
from the present since I was a child. My education has
affirmed that my capacity for deconstruction is central to
my intelligence.

At LAX customs, there was a blank space on the wall
where Obama's portrait had hung. Trump's face still hadn't
replaced it. Waiting to go through border patrol, I replayed
Zoya's voice saying "they're asleep," saying "overwhelm
me," saying my name. Grace. It lost its history when she
said it, became something new.

I looked down at my passport. Grace Dunham. Female.
Five foot ten. Born January 28, 1992. Fake smile, thick

glasses, ponytail. Female. Who was she kidding? I didn't even believe myself.

A Lyft driver named Rick pulled up outside the terminal in a white Prius, his iPhone scotch-taped to the dashboard. The back seat was full of books.

"Feel free," he said, "to take a look at the books. Look through them all."

All the books had his face on the cover, smiling, a little off-center. The titles were printed in sans serif: *The Art of Thinking*, volumes 1, 2, 3, and 4. "Rick is an enlightened artist, novelist, and musician who follows no man's rules and truly marches to the beat of his own drum," the bio read.

"Cool stuff, eh?" he asked.

He kept turning around at stoplights to tell me things: he'd changed many women's lives; they'd sobbed in the back seat, broken down, kissed the top of his head, asked if he was an angel.

Somewhere in Baldwin Hills, he asked, "Do you think you're real, girl?"

"I don't know, Rick." The answer, of course, was that I did not feel real. Not in the slightest. The only thing that felt real to me was my all-consuming desire to return to the childhood bedroom of the girl I'd just spent two weeks with, whom I felt was the guardian of my becoming.

"You're not real, girl," said the enlightened artist. "We're just plugged in. Holograms in an ectoplasmic network created by the architects, the archangels. This is a game, girl. Play it.

"What do you think, girl?" he said. "What do you think?"

What I thought was that I wanted a wall of manhood around me. I was sick of being porous to all new positions and incapable of not empathizing.

We neared my neighborhood. Off the highway, past the IHOP, turning on Cypress, toward the river, up San Fernando, closer and closer to home. We turned onto Future Street.

"Listen, you're cool, I want to give you a gift."

He handed me a screen-printed CD. His face smiled up at me. A CD of love songs.

"Enjoy it. Listen closely. Peace, Grace. Peace."

After he drove away, I threw the CD in the trash.

Hearing him say the name Grace disgusted me. I unlocked the door, went up to my room, threw my luggage on the floor, and pulled the picture of Zoya and me out of its envelope. I held it by the edges, tilting it so the sunlight bounced off different parts of Zoya's body. Then I looked at my yellow notepad, where I'd written down, four times: "Don't turn me into a fiction. Don't turn me into a fiction. Don't turn me into a fiction. Don't turn me into a fiction." Eight thousand six hundred eighty-eight miles away from her, Zoya seemed hyperreal. Without her, my sense of self dissipated. The fiction was me.

2

THE WEEK I RETURNED to Los Angeles, I dreamed I had anesthetic awareness during top surgery. My eyes were closed and I couldn't move. I felt the surgeon sliding fat and glands out from under the incisions, leaving empty pouches where my breasts had been, then stitching the flaps of skin back down to my chest muscles. The combination of immobility and consciousness wasn't so terrifying. I breathed into the sharpness of the feeling as they finished closing me up and was calm.

In the dream I woke up groggy. The procedure had been its own trancelike dream within the dream. After, I sat slumped over in a wheelchair, eyes a quarter open. I wore a compression top velcroed around my chest to keep the skin down. It kept me inside myself, a tight hug. A stranger wheeled me through a hallway into a waiting room.

Then I was in the lobby of my high school: grand, red-carpeted staircase, marble floor, classical Greek statues cast in plaster framing the entryway. Circles of girls whispered, and circles of boys messed around with each other, their backpacks slung over one shoulder. A few pubescent couples sat on the bottom steps, holding each other's hands with awkward purposefulness.

I leaned back against the wall in an oversized army-green T-shirt and baggy blue jeans. They hung on me, as if my mom had gotten them with extra room for me to grow into. I wasn't hunched over, but I still felt concave. My arms were at my sides, not crossed over my chest in a protective X. I ran my fingers through my hair. It was thick and a little stiff. I looked down at my fingers. They were long, rough. The veins on the backs of my hands popped out. A muscle in my forearm twitched when I moved my thumb. I felt an energy stored in my back, my shoulders, my biceps; if I needed to pull myself up, or push myself over something, I'd be able to. I loped from one side of the lobby to the other, the bottoms of my jeans dragging under my shoes. Loose and limber, I moved gently. My body worked. Relief. So much relief. I let myself believe this was a permanent state of being.

I woke up from the dream in my bed in Los Angeles, expecting strength and flatness. Lying on my back, adjusting to the morning light, I slung one arm under my head, reached down with the other to scratch my chest. My hands felt small, like a child's. They found breasts. Lumps between me and myself, between me and whomever I wanted to feel against my chest, between me and the world. The thing about these appendages was that, even though everyone I'd ever slept with assured me they were especially good tits, to me they were utter surplus. One lover had commented on the perky, upright optimism with which the nipples pointed toward the heavens. This made me develop a habit of stretching the nipples as far as I could toward the ground, until they looked like those pink cusk eels that live in the bottom of the ocean, slithering without sunlight.

I could never, once the breasts started to grow, see them as a permanent part of me. It seemed like if I pricked them with a needle or cut a slit at the bottom of each sack, all the excess liquid should drain out and the skin should pull itself taut again, back against my ribs, where it belonged. I imagined that the seeping liquid would be white and thick, like the mucus that gathers on the stems of milky sap plants, all the food of the hypothetical children I would never have gathering on the floor below me in a puddle. Better there than inside of me.

I flipped over onto my stomach, the flesh-mounds underneath me, and wrapped my pillow around my head. Loss, dread, betrayal. All-encompassing disappointment filling in the space made by longing. Without someone next to me to hold, I had to face my own body.

Zoya had been distant. She had warned me this might happen but that I shouldn't take it as a sign of her diminishing love. Nonetheless, within seventy-two hours of returning home, I'd begun writing the script of my own rejection, just as she'd cautioned me not to. And, to make the script bearable, I'd reverted to—or, more accurately, marched on with—some of my preferred coping strategies: alcohol, ketamine, cocaine, anything that was available. Substances, whatever their effects, melted my masterful, forensic analysis of every moment into an indiscernible sludge. When I was sober, I surveilled myself. My sentences, my twitches, my limbs, my hand motions, the way I gasped for air at the end of a sentence. At least, if I was sludge, I could relax. Uppers and downers, as different as their outcomes might be, have a shared strength, which is their ability to take you either over or under yourself, until you're far enough away that you don't have to *be* yourself at all. Or whoever you've convinced yourself you are.

When Zoya did call me, it was at strange hours: five a.m. her time, after a night she hadn't slept. She told me she'd looked at apartments in Mumbai and found one near the sea, where she'd put a desk in front of the window. She thought I'd like sitting there. She kept the logistics of our reunion abstract. I pushed toward concrete planning. Could she visit me in June? Could I come see her? I'd have more money soon; I'd buy a plane ticket. I'd come for the summer. Maybe I'd stay.

I'd been cycling through our two and a half weeks

together on repeat, looking for clues as to whether what happened between us was more than just a convincing hallucination. Looking for signs that I could continue to be the person she desired even when I was away from her. I still had heightened sensation in the spots where she touched me: the back of my neck, the tops of my shoulders, my forearms. She had made them radiate some kind of warm, tingling potential. I hated myself for still believing that one person, a lover, could rid me of whatever kept me hating myself in the first place.

I kept the printed picture of us from the photo studio in its white envelope, hidden in between books. The ritual of taking the picture out of the envelope grew increasingly masochistic: instead of reminding me I had existed alongside her, it made me that much more aware of her absence.

It's not that I hadn't been in love, or in pain, before. I met Antonia when I was twenty, and six years later we were still entangled, neither technically together nor wholly apart.

Antonia had big owl eyes, and her pupils dilated when she focused on something. She was also a photographer, like my mother, which gave her gaze a particular power. Her beauty pulled at something ancient in me, provoked an urgency that made all previous desire seem manageable in comparison.

The first time we met, she stared at me as if I was hiding something. I still had long hair then, which I kept out of my face with bobby pins. I was still a young democrat and a young woman. She appeared to know something about me that I didn't yet have language for.

As things progressed, Antonia never called me pretty or beautiful. She intuited what would be most uncomfortable and necessary for me to hear.

"You're not a girl," she'd say. "You're too handsome."

It seemed like if I followed her, I'd end up somewhere I'd always assumed was off-limits to me: a place where people externalized their desires without ambivalence.

Early in our relationship, Antonia started photographing me. Never all of me, just parts of my body, isolated in the frame. My elbow, chest, foot, or knee, alongside objects she'd collected and anthropomorphized: a bone, a burnt fan, an ax, a rose. She'd print the images, then distort the pictures by burning, freezing, or bleaching them. Once the final image was complete, I was illegible; another component in an abstracted surface. In the final image, the visible parts of me barely looked human, let alone female. Submitting to her vision was a home, of sorts. I was something abstract in her eyes, something more mercurial than girlhood.

When I found the courage to ask Antonia if she was having sex with other people, she told me desire was not a scarce resource. I set out to prove to her—but mostly to myself—that I agreed. I lost my ability to sleep, spending the night in half-dream hazes of her fucking men, women, and creatures that made her feel things I never would, never could. When I suspected she'd been with someone else, I vomited, then said things like, "I'm in pain, but I would never want you to limit yourself because of me. Trust that I know my own limits." Really, I was sick with jealousy. This jealousy registered in my body as it had when I was a teenager and I saw a girl I fixated on directing her attention toward a boy. Antonia affirmed that her devotion was unwavering, made space for all my paranoia. But I couldn't explain away the fear that she didn't love me, that someone else—anyone more masculine than I was—would replace me.

Previously, I had understood myself as sane, insofar as I hid my perversions underneath my high-achieving-blazer-wearing-female-debate-champion-with-a-side-braid persona. As a child and an adolescent, I developed compulsive strategies for suppressing my preoccupations. When I longed to kiss or tie up girls, I recited the provinces of Canada, or ranked the most famous European modernists, or made lists of cities with each new one starting with the last letter of the one before it. Information calmed me down. There was so much to know. The more I knew, the more special I'd be. Gropius, Corbusier, Alvar Aalto, Mies van der Rohe. Saint Petersburg–Guadalajara–Ankara–Asmara–Arezzo–Osaka–Amman. British Columbia, Alberta, Saskatchewan, Manitoba, Ontario, Quebec, Newfoundland, and Labrador. West to East and back again. I reminded myself I'd be something great when I grew up. I would hide my visions and build great buildings instead, or I'd build great enough buildings that the visions wouldn't matter. I drew homes partially built into hillsides or suspended off cliffs hanging over the oceans. Museums, government offices, and hospitals as beautiful as they were practical. I pictured big, clean, open rooms I'd shaped. Everyone would feel important and clean inside of them. Light would pour in from all sides. I imagined an apartment where there was nothing around me I hadn't chosen on purpose, because it meant something or because it was beautiful. I imagined a closet full of suits, organized by color.

Soon after I fell in love with Antonia, all the pushed-down pain erupted. Every moment I had ever believed I was unlovable seemed to rise, such that I was utterly inconsolable about betrayals she had yet to enact on me. She stayed, trying to help me understand what I couldn't yet say.

Two years into our relationship, Antonia and I dated someone together, Stella. She wore red lipstick and lots of black lace. She bought slices of raw steak at the butcher shop in the morning and ate them with her coffee. When we met, shitfaced in a rooftop hotel swimming pool, surrounded by bankers, the first thing I asked her was what she did, which was make music; the second thing I asked her was whether she wanted to be famous. (I was always blacking out and asking people about fame, then. I needed to know they could be honest about the power it had over them, over everyone.) She said no. Two days later was Antonia's birthday, and the three of us had confusing sex in my parents' bed, on top of the same pink sheets where I'd had sex for the first time.

In the subsequent configuration, I fluctuated between

jealousy and euphoria. When I slept between Antonia and Stella, I felt an abundant safety for which I had no language. Three was a family; at times, it seemed unbreakable. But if I woke up to them embracing, I spiraled into existential dread. Seeing my partner, my supposed anchor, sleeping peacefully in the arms of another person—this was a loss not only of security, but of identity.

Our first fall together, the three of us went to Maine, to the town where Stella had spent her adolescence. We drove around in her car, an old Mercedes coupe; I didn't have a license yet, but they let me drive the twisty country roads anyway. We drove to a field where we walked through shoulder-height goldenrods. On the other side of a pine forest there was a cliff next to a lake. The three of us had sex on the rocks and I scraped my knees. After, I slid down into the water. I swam backward, away from them. They started to have sex again without me. The water was cold and it numbed my skin. Watching them, I stopped having a body. I was the water and the water was me. If I wasn't me, there was nothing to be afraid of. No one could leave me or stop loving me. I didn't exist, and so I wasn't Grace. I wanted to stay watching them in the water into infinity.

Along the way, I fell in love with Stella, too. In her company, my body was less constraining. I noticed myself making bigger gestures, moving without fear of my own clumsiness.

My devotion split in two. I split in two as well. Afraid

to risk losing the love of either of them—and the sense of self summoned by each—I clung to them both, managing simultaneous realities that could not coexist.

Ultimately, Antonia and I stayed together. But more and more people in my life began to accuse me of dishonesty. My mother told me I had a lying bone. A friend who had caught on to my habit gave me her marked-up copy of a 1975 Adrienne Rich essay called "Women and Honor: Some Notes on Lying." Rich writes that the liars, afraid of themselves, cannot bear their own contradictions, cannot face what might be lost if they are honest.

I said whatever I thought people wanted to hear. I'll be there at seven p.m. sharp. Yes, Saturday works. No, I love you and only you. I'm certain. I desire no one else. I'm hungry. I'm not hungry. I miss you. I need you too. I want to come. I'm coming. I just came. I'm sorry. I'm not angry with you, and I don't resent you. I couldn't lie to you. I didn't lie. I didn't lie. I didn't lie. I didn't lie about lying.

Calling something a lie implies that one has the truth in one's mouth and swallows it. What if one can only speak— only think—what one suspects another person wants to hear? Then where is the truth? How does one learn to think it?

The more I suspected people thought I was a liar, the more impossible it seemed to tell the "truth." There were so many truths; I didn't know how to locate one. Lying was embedded in every gesture, every statement, every inter- action; every time I reaffirmed the presumption that I was female, which was constantly. I resigned myself to being in-capable of not lying. To do otherwise would require being a new person entirely, one who had not fashioned themself—"herself"—around hiding.

I felt continually closer to unraveling each day back in Los Angeles, each day that Zoya seemed more like an appari-tion. Random things made me cry. The person dressed as the Liberty Tax mascot on the corner of La Brea and Pico. An old woman in a purple gown pushing an empty stroller. A sign outside a boarded-up turquoise bungalow that said "Institute for Levity." A fucking hummingbird. Everything burst with meaning. Everything was a mouth about to swallow me.

I couldn't interact with anyone or anything without ab-sorbing their feelings—or, more accurately, what I perceived to be their feelings. A hybrid sponge-sail, I sucked it all up, then lost my course. I wanted harder skin, better bound-aries, interconnectedness without losing myself. I hated my body, even though I could hardly feel it.

I hesitate to call the exhausting day-to-day of embodi-ment "dysphoria," that catchall for the pain of having a body that doesn't align with one's sense of self. What was a sense of self, after all: a delusion; mental illness. I struggled to believe my own discomfort. I just felt crazy. And if I admitted I was dysphoric, I'd have to deal with the fallout. I'd have to decide whether to do something about it.

In its most basic definition, dysphoria simply means

"a state of unease." The unease was far-reaching. I was vapor trapped in a container. The bugs I held hostage in Tupperware when I was a child. A windowless room with no doors, a single dangling light that never turned off, no beginning and no end. An eternity without sunlight, a breeze, moisture, the crickets chirping through the window. Coming to in a shut coffin, six feet underground, shrieking at graveyard earth. Waking up on Pluto, perched on its gray curve, the galaxy in front of you, unreachable. The ocean underneath Antarctica, entirely encased by ice. Rising to the underside of a frozen lake, sealed off but pounding. Never being touched. Never being spoken to. Never being looked at. Claustrophobia in perpetuity; isolation in infinitude; the body experienced as every metaphor for confinement.

How to know if the problem was gender or personhood. How to know if the problem was gender or me.

This was where drinking came in. It melted me, postponed the question of whether I needed to be an active agent in escaping my own bodily claustrophobia. When, as a teenager, I started binge drinking on the weekends, I woke up with foggy memories: a boy's tongue in my mouth; his hand down my pants; vomiting. The memories of a regular girl, having fun. I hadn't enacted them; I had drunk and so they had happened to me.

The first time I got high was in the woods in Prospect Park. A group of boys had showed a group of girls how to inhale and keep the smoke inside long enough. It was September, still warm, and I was dressed up in a three-tiered baby-blue miniskirt. At first I didn't feel anything, just the sting of the smoke in my lungs. Then my eyes started throbbing in my skull. I was wearing tight goggles and being a teenager was a video game. Everyone else was real. The boys were handsome, happy, and full of laughter. The girls wanted their approval. Each boy was a main character, an amalgamation of characteristics that rendered him a leading man. Letting men be protagonists was indulgent and pornographic. It was not what I'd been taught. It was nasty, backward, even medieval. The more I tried to block the boys from becoming protagonists, the more I succumbed to the storyline. Until his hands were my hands, his feet were my feet, his dick was my dick. The story always ended with him—with me as him or in him—seated in a chair, head back and eyes closed, moaning in ecstasy, a girl's mouth around me. The scene throbbed in the back of my eyelids, begging for completion, for ejaculation.

I went into the trees and lay down on the ground. It was cold and I had goose bumps all over my skin. But my body wasn't real so the cold didn't matter much. The skinny, breast-budding, miniskirted pale thing was just a container. I focused on my heartbeat and felt it pushing blood through my body. I felt the blood sloshing around inside me, hot at the edges of the container. I looked down and saw a dirty little skirt and gangly stick legs. When I closed my eyes I felt the blood forming into an extension of myself, long and hard, lifting up from between my legs. I felt the tip of myself radiating heat and numbness, an ache in the base of my back that curled my spine and toes. I counted to sixty-four, pushing the tingling feeling further out into the extension at each number. I counted to sixty-four again. Soon the numbers were so close together that they stopped being separate. Then I was hollow, a porcelain casting of a person, filled with liquid light. The cast shattered. There was no container.

After that I became addicted to the splitting feeling. It hurt a little, and I knew that when it hurt my body cracked and I wasn't me anymore. It was just a few seconds but the crack was so big that it got me through the day, knowing I'd get to split again at night. I lay in the dark on my back and counted to eight, 1, 2, 3, 4, 5, 6, 7, 8. Eight times. If I got too close to the crack I stopped and stepped back; at sixty-four, I let it swallow me. It was like this for a while, just counting until I let the painful ache get huge, until I figured out that I could pair it with the visions I'd made in my head since I was little. I used class, when I was supposed to be paying attention, and the subway ride to and from school, and the walk from the train to my house, and the elevator ride, and every other moment I was alone and undisturbed, to visualize the scenes, down to the colors, individual touches, and dialogue, then play them in my head like movies. I was never in the movies, because I wasn't compelled by myself as a character. Usually, the star was a young, handsome, kind boy. He was pale and lean, but strong. Soft-spoken, but severe. He had thick brown hair and thick eyebrows, and posture that made him curl like a question mark. Sometimes he was with an older woman; sometimes, an older man. They coveted him and he lay there like a baby when they touched him, overwhelmed by how much they wanted to hold him.

A few weeks after I got back from India, I started having panic attacks again. Deep, rolling ones that hit hard and then came back smaller, again and again. The rhythm of panic was oceanic. I stayed still, letting the swell run its course, resigned to the fact that I might not emerge.

I had my first debilitating panic attack in the bathroom of a midtown theater, at a premiere celebrating the release of my sister's television show. I was wearing a light gray suit that had previously been my father's. My first suit. In the lobby of the theater people grabbed at me and asked me how proud I was. "So, so proud," I'd say. "Couldn't be prouder." I was as angry about fame worship as I was guilty of it. I hadn't learned any other way to be.

I sat in the audience between my parents while a young woman spoke onstage in a beautiful dress provided for the occasion. The walls of the theater were red and gold. She made jokes and the crowd laughed in a joint roar. The woman onstage, from a distance, shared many physical traits and speech patterns with the person whom I knew as my older sister. It was an effective hologram, a convincing depiction of a smart-but-humble, funny-yet-earnest young woman. A rosy-cheeked, lovable daughter of the audience. On my right, a striking, gray-haired man in a trim suit and thick-framed glasses sat with his hands folded on his lap. He looked like my father. The elegant redheaded woman known as my mother sat on the other side of me, clutching my hands with her long, pale fingers, her red manicure. I was supposed to know and love them, swell with pride for the woman onstage. Either they were imposters or I was a sociopath. The theater was an opaque box with no exits and it was rapidly running out of air. Being a daughter was a show was a myth was a commodity was a white lie was a dream was a movie.

The panic attack announced itself in this way: at first, the sped-up, echoing voice of Amelia Earhart, my narrative ghost, calling out to me. White aliens, she was saying. White aliens. White aliens. White aliens. The words made it hard to breathe. I had the acute feeling that no one I was looking at was real. White aliens taught other aliens to succeed at all costs, to put the dissemination of one's own message above all else. White aliens taught white aliens that to die alone or a nobody was the worst thing a woman could do.

I went to the women's restroom, which was empty, and entered the large corner stall, where I vomited up water and popcorn and collapsed onto the floor hyperventilating. I wondered if I was having a heart attack. I couldn't breathe and I clutched at my chest. Clawed at it. It occurred to me that my body was not mine. Neither was my brain. Grace? Who is Grace? I was a cloud stuck inside a person I didn't choose to be.

At some point the sobs subsided. I splashed water on

my face. I went back to the theater. I explained away my momentary break as the product of my burgeoning political consciousness. I was learning concepts to explain why the world around me looked the way it did: money hungry, fame driven, alienated, and bereft of care. Naturally, I was having physical reactions.

Afterward there was a party. I drank. People talked to me and I answered, the good student that I was. *College is wonderful. I'm really enjoying my classes. Yes, I'm dating someone, an artist. I'm so endlessly proud of my sister. It's a lot to live up to but I'm just glad she's getting to live out her dreams. I'm not sure what I want to do. I'm interested in a lot of things. Journalism, politics, law. I agree, it is important that there be visible gay women in power.*

That night at Antonia's, she fell asleep and I stayed up, curled in a ball on the floor. The more I tried to stop crying the more I hyperventilated. It occurred to me that I'd never been real. I recalled being a child and the memories felt as if they'd been implanted, pictures downloaded into a manufactured brain. That was a nice time, being young in a small world. That was a nice time, getting to be a child. I heard myself talking to Antonia, sobbing; it was the voice of a little girl who wished she was a boy.

After that night, the sorrow bubbled up from its unnameable source more and more often. First, just at night. Then also during the day. Soon, in explosions of anxiety that swallowed up whole weeks.

The more disoriented I became, the more I clung to Antonia.

If I found the right words to tell her where I was, why I was there, she could pull me out of isolation, keep me close to her. I remember sitting on her bed, hunched over while she stood looking down at me, just telling her it hurt, over and over. I couldn't tell her what the it was because I didn't know.

Unable to contain my frenzy of need, I wrote Zoya a scathing email accusing her of hiding from my love. I thought I was being brave and honest. In retrospect, I was just being desperate. She wrote back, a day later, a gentle and measured interrogation of my entitlement to her emotions, of my unseemly, and particularly American, impatience.

Ashamed, I went to a party. I needed to be sated by something, though I didn't know what. In a warehouse between two industrial neighborhoods, the party was full of hundreds of shirtless, mostly white gay men. I did ketamine and coke. Rather than relaxing into euphoria, I was engulfed by envy for the homogeneity of their bodies—the V-lines where their lower abdomens met their obliques; their visible triceps muscles; the shadows underneath their protruding pecs. The men appeared to be dancing with their own twins. Slight mutations of the Mark Wahlberg genus. The substances in my bloodstream heightened my awareness of the testosterone in theirs. Sculpting, chiseling, hardening, and enhancing them. Estrogen dominant, I would melt and soften until I turned to liquid, milk on the floor.

Back when boys started going through puberty, I kept lists in my mind of which ones had hair under their arms and above their lips. The ones who got hair first started looking stronger, too. They weren't so scrawny anymore. Those same boys got extra-sweaty and smelled bad. That was all because of testosterone. Some of them even had lines on their abdomens, or biceps that bulged when they pulled a textbook off the shelf. When their shirts were made of thin, soft cotton, you could see their muscles through the cloth. When I was alone in front of the mirror, I copied some of the movements the boys did in gym class—throwing their hands up in frustration, clapping to get another player's attention, hitting their fists against their chests when they were happy, knocking their heads back when they were frustrated. I did the movements and watched how the cloth of my shirt caught on my skin.

I lost my sense of linear time and found myself on the stage at the front of the party, a plywood and paint re-creation of the Oval Office, hung with portraits of Trump and his cabinet, splattered with white paint and glue meant to look like jiz.

A man I didn't know grabbed me and kissed me. "It's a bukkake show," he said.

Bukkake. Milk. Mark Wahlberg. The White House. Aliens. All aliens. I could either be part of the sea of white men or let dissociation vaporize me, turn me into a nano-particle of condensation floating into the oblivion.

Orbs of dislodged emotion levitated above the ground. Claustrophobia. Dread. Loneliness. Infinite, already-failed solutions. A lonely ghost who can't cease to be itself. The men became floating cubes, backed by blue light. What's the difference between a man and a box, anyway?

At some point I dragged myself through the warehouse to the outdoor port-a-potties. Inside the port-a-potty I tried to pee standing up. Piss drizzled down my legs, onto the gray plastic ledge around the toilet. Then either the lock got stuck or I couldn't figure out how to open it, so I slammed myself against the door. One, two, three slams. The port-a-potty started to tip over. I got out mid-tumble, watched it swing back and forth, wavy, until it reached standing position and was sturdy again.

The next day, unable to get out of bed, I called my best friend Jessica and admitted to needing her. She came over, made me shower, laid a blanket over me, forced me to eat, and fed me a corner shard of Klonopin, splitting the rest of the pill up into three pieces and wrapping them in tinfoil.

She was my oldest friend. As teenagers, we both believed we were disgusting, albeit for different reasons. She was one of those beautiful girls who believed she was rotten. The distance between our interiors and exteriors bonded us to each other. Back then we rode the train home from school together every day, getting off at the same stop and standing on a street corner talking until it was dark out. I thought about coming out to her for many years before I finally did. She was the only person to whom telling the truth seemed at all possible. But I couldn't get the words out. They sat in my throat, stuck. When I finally told her, the confession pulled the seal off my solitude. She is, perhaps, the only person I've allowed to watch me change. Thus, she is the only one who knows my continuity. I'd like to think we provide coherence for each other and, in doing so, make changing safer.

She's always been the one to both schedule and escort me to obligatory appointments—the DMV, the cognitive behavioral therapist, the gynecologist.

"You know this is about you," she said. "Not Zoya."

She told me my obsessions were a stand-in for what I didn't wish to look at in myself. I knew she was right and I also resented her scrutiny. I wanted her to let me be in love, let me use that in-love-ness as a compass so I could pretend I had direction. The hope of pretending is that, with enough time and practice, the performance becomes you.

That night I sat on the floor of my room and wrote a list of New Year's resolutions on a piece of pink printer paper I'd found on the carpet at Staples, even though it was already March.

1. Less alcohol.
2. Don't lie.
3. Don't make decisions from a place of panic.
4. Keep your nails short so you can't pick scabs on your head.
5. Spend more time alone.
6. Don't seek out lovers to fix you.
7. Be honest with your family about your gender, whatever that means.
8. Be honest with yourself about your gender, whatever that means.

3

I WASN'T EXPECTING to hear from Anna. We hadn't spoken in a year and a half. Anna and I met when I was eighteen and she was twenty-two. At the time, she was still using the name and pronouns she'd been assigned at birth. She'd been one of my best friends; then we kept hurting each other until neither one of us knew what to apologize for anymore. Now, out of the blue, an email from her:

i have been thinking about you a lot for different reasons.
  i have been doing big work around my gender, trying to answer some of the things you asked me about in the past. i feel like to be concrete i would need volumes with you—may we get that.

I'd heard through friends that she was no longer identifying as a man. The last time we'd seen each other it was freezing and we'd sat on a bench in Washington Square Park. I asked her, again, why she was living as a man if she didn't feel like one. She'd wished she was a woman since she was a child. She'd softly told me, again, that she felt a sense of responsibility: to be a good man, a kind man, a self-aware man. This angered me, though I was equally beholden to womanhood at the time. But in my map of the world, the map I'd been given, manhood was something to reject and womanhood was something to extol. I wanted her to rid herself of her manhood so that I could stop envying her and disdaining her in equal parts. When she didn't, I resigned myself to our drifting apart. Apathy was a much less painful place to be than grief or anger.

Nonetheless, when she emailed me, all the missing came rushing back in. So much had happened, so much we hadn't spoken about. I wrote back right away telling her to visit me. She took a long weekend off work and booked a ticket from Philadelphia to LAX.

Months before we ever spoke, I saw her lying in the grass in a blousy, open shirt, with a beautiful, severe-looking young woman. The woman held Anna's head in her hands like a baby's. Anna reached her hands up, her fingers tangled in the woman's brown hair. They rolled around in the grass, books scattered around them. I projected unparalleled brilliance, self-possession, and fulfillment onto the scene. Anna still publicly identified with her assigned gender then. She had strong hands, a triangle of soft hair above her sternum visible through a gauzy white button-down. She was beautiful and poised. I walked around the rest of the day imagining myself in her body, as I often did with young men (or apparent young men) I admired.

That winter, she introduced herself to me at a crowded party in a basement. Her dead name, the name she was given at birth, was a lofty one, from the Old Testament. I thought it suited her even though it would later seem unimaginable. We went from one party to another, then drove to a beach outside the city and talked until the early morning. I hadn't met a boy before who listened to me the way she did. She asked me open questions about my family and my friends, about my interests, about my sexuality.

I thought about her in the following days. I tried to visualize kissing her, being naked next to her. But in the fantasies I slipped into her body: her forearms became my forearms; her chest became my chest; her hands became my hands.

She'd grown up in a book-filled farmhouse on the edge of an industrial city in central Massachusetts, where her Marxist parents had raised her to be suspicious of beauty, aware of its relationship to power. She wasn't impressed by success in its own right: meritocracy was a myth, determined by access to resources. This destabilized my own story, the comfort I took in achievement, how I used it to protect myself against my shame. Her frameworks made the world into a new and unfamiliar landscape.

Around the same time we met, my sister started getting famous. I saw it on the horizon before it actually happened: attention and opportunities drawing the outlines of a public space for her to step into. I saw her about to be swallowed and repurposed by a large machine, the intricate processes that Anna had made more transparent to me. Fame was a toxic substance that oozed into everything. People acted strangely when they knew they were near it. They wanted it and they revered it, but it also hurt them. It stuck to everything it touched, like sap. If you wanted to get rid of it, you had to amputate the part of you it was adhered to. At least, these were my paranoias. Anna didn't treat fame like a triumph. She asked me about my grief and fear, let there be something to mourn. I was angry, scared of losing my sister, troubled that everyone assumed I was jealous and even more troubled that I might be.

Anna watched my anxiety overtake me and, as a result, grew more diligent in her care. She made it clear my de-pression didn't lessen her love for me. She drove to Rhode Island often to see me and lay next to me in bed while I cried and didn't speak. I was learning that the organizing principle of her life—or, at least, the goal she strived for— was something more collective than I'd previously been exposed to. She saw more value in friends lying next to one another, with no clear goal in mind, than she did in the singular pursuits that often constitute success. As fame pulled my sister further into its machinations, and mental illness pulled me further into its swamp, I needed a new system to make sense of my pain. It was much easier to be critical than it was to feel loss. Beliefs seemed like better justification for anger than simple, inexplicable sadness. Anna supplied something like a new belief system: she didn't celebrate what I'd been taught to celebrate.

At that time, my closest friends except for Jessica were young men; white, Jewish ones from major American cities who had gone to elite private schools, like myself. My adolescence had been a practice in reserved control; I had a tight grip on my id, never let it make itself known. With these young men, I had to explode to keep up.

They got me to break things and drink until I threw up, jump off cliffs into bodies of water. When they were angry, it was direct; they were sad when I didn't show up the way I'd said I would. We often fell asleep in piles, like bears, and even though I didn't like the way they smelled, it was an accomplishment to be one of them. Plus, they cherished me. And while this disgusted me, it also enabled my superiority, the primary means through which I convinced myself I didn't envy them. Samuel, with whom I was closest, analyzed his own patterns with psychoanalytic mastery, then continued on brazenly, unchanging. I kept him close so I could gather evidence for just how different we were. At the same time, I studied him, selectively mirroring.

Anna, unlike Samuel, was gentle, even effeminate. I couldn't rationalize my superiority by dismissing her as a brute. She seemed at ease with words, with beliefs, with choices, with lovers. She became a voice in my head, like

71

Amelia Earhart before her; when she wasn't there, I heard her holding forth, a disembodied observer assessing my value in every moment. When I couldn't sleep, I catalogued her insights and opinions, her intonation rolling over my consciousness.

When I met Antonia, she remarked that Anna and I were similar. Was this why I worshipped her? Was she a more evolved version of me? The better one?

I was sure that if Anna and I were pitted against each other in Antonia's eyes, I would lose. I succumbed to apocalyptic fantasies of heterosexual sex between them, passionate and focused, charged with an intensity I could never reach. Every time Antonia told me they'd seen each other, I got off the phone woozy. I saw myself from the outside, crouching at a distance, watching them exist in their fullness. The only thing I had over Anna was that I, unlike her, was a woman. And women were superior. This, I had been taught. This, I knew.

I picked Anna up at LAX. I saw her from a distance, hunched over in black leggings and a long black T-shirt, her hair dyed blond, grown out to her shoulders. I jumped out of my car and we hugged for a long time, without saying anything.

We drove to the beach and lay on a big blue blanket in the sand. We ran into the Pacific in our underwear. It was freezing. She'd always been able to convince me to swim in cold water. Perhaps because I wanted to keep up; perhaps because she made it seem meaningful. She's always looking out for heightened experiences, anything that makes two people feel closer together: drugs, matching tattoos, jumping in the freezing ocean. We ran back up to our blanket and lay in the sun, our arms under our heads and our legs crossed, mirroring each other. Our hair was similar in length, falling loose at our shoulders, and our bodies were more similar than they'd ever been before. Her edges had softened somewhat, and mine had hardened.

A few days after she arrived, we drove the six hours from Los Angeles to the Bay Area, where Anna was visiting friends in Richmond. I'd agreed to drop her off, then experiment with "doing my own thing." The I-5 is a death trail; it drops down into the Central Valley, past Ikea's distribution center, through industrial farms, maximum-security prisons, and former Japanese internment camps. There's one part of the ride that encases you in the smell of manure ammonia and dead flesh; on either side, hundreds of thousands of cows feed and drink from dark brown pools of brackish water. People call this ranch "Cowschwitz."

Halfway through the trip, when it was already dark, Anna told me that she had her first dose of estrogen in her suitcase. She'd gone to a clinic in Philadelphia before leaving. She'd been waiting, seeing what it felt like to know the substance was in her possession.

My discomfort cut through the conversation. I got dizzy, heard my thoughts as a foreign voice, lost track of the road until I realized I was driving thirty miles per hour under the speed limit.

I heard my voice performing congratulations, selfless support, compersion (a neologism born out of polyamory, which Anna had taught me, meaning "the feeling of joy one has experiencing another's joy," or the opposite of jealousy). But I yawned involuntarily, pulling in oxygen to mitigate the dizziness. My face got hot and my fingers and toes numbed. My response was too physiological for me to locate one emotion.

Rapid-fire, I attempted to logic my way out of incapacity with calming evidence:

(A) Anna was not braver than me for beginning hormone replacement therapy. (B) Estrogen would make her body curvier and I wouldn't have to envy her shape the way I did now. (C) I didn't need hormonal therapy to legitimize my gender nonconformity. (D) Physical transition was more urgent for her, because to be a transfeminine person in public is to be harassed, mocked, and watched in ways I'd never been and would never be. (E) She could medically transition and I could stay looking like a woman but knowing I wasn't and the two didn't cancel each other out. (F) There is no scarcity, there is no scarcity, there is no scarcity, there is no scarcity.

Most important: Anna's voyage was a righteous and divine one, toward the manifestation of her femininity. Becoming a woman: this I could understand, celebrate, defend.

Since I'd moved to LA, I'd scheduled multiple appointments at LGBTQ clinics to get testosterone. Each time, I found some reason not to show up. The drive was too far; I didn't have the proper paperwork; I'd changed my mind. It was unclear to me what the act of scheduling the appointments even meant to me. I didn't plan on telling anyone, just imagined a gradual squaring out in my jaw, becoming a little leaner, stopping before I grew any hair on my face or body and brushing the changes off as natural. But the closer I got to the appointment, the more disgusting the potentialities of the process seemed. Facial hair, body hair, fat redistribution, mood change, clitoral enlargement, change in body odor. I could fathom some of these as isolated changes, but together they added up to something grotesque and terrifying. How could anyone else love me if I was disgusted by myself? The knowledge that I wasn't a woman was all that mattered, I told myself. If I could withstand my body without altering it, if I could will it to work for me, I would be strong.

Anna and I had been talking throughout my internal lecture. I don't remember what we talked about. I flipped back into presentness when she told me she'd chosen a new name.

"Anna," she said.

Anna, the name of the brown-haired five-year-old who wore a pink bow in her hair and whom I kissed in the back corner of the classroom. Anna the palindrome. Anna, Anna, Anna, Anna.

I dropped Anna off on the outskirts of Richmond, then drove north to a town where the Russian River empties out into the Pacific. From the cliffs above the ocean you could see the brown river water spilling into the blue ocean water, mixing together. No slow, sandy fade like the Atlantic coast, just cliffs, cut off, then the sea.

I spent the next day walking around the town, which consisted of one gas station, until the sun set and I bought a six-pack to drink in my extremely damp motel room. I called Zoya a few times; she didn't answer. I called Antonia, who attempted to comfort me by reminding me that she hadn't gone anywhere, that we still loved each other, if in a different form. Still, I was certain neither she nor Zoya needed me anymore. And if neither one of them needed me, I was no one. I sobbed, sadness bubbling up from the irrational, indescribable place. It was easiest to call it heartbreak and reach for different objects in the shape of people.

The sun set and I drank until I slept. The four hours until a reasonable bedtime seemed infinite and unnavigable. I could not stand to be self-aware. I drank until I didn't even notice I was unconscious.

I woke up early the next morning, dehydrated and angry at Anna. I wouldn't tell her about or show her my anger; I'd celebrate the work she'd done to get to this point. I would show up for her, just as she'd taught me, as she leaped the bureaucratic hurdles of name and gender change: email addresses, bank cards, IDs, online accounts. People from the past would be notified of the new name, either by her or by an acquaintance, and they'd overperform their comfort with it to prove how okay they were with the transformation.

I'd protect her even though I envied her, even though envy begets resentment. Why was I so slow?

I was slow because the very idea of "transitioning"—starting hormones, getting surgery, even just changing my name—sucked me into a thought circuit with no end and no exits: I need this. The fact that I need this means I'm weak. The fact that I'm weak means I don't deserve this. I need this.

I went to a beach famous for sea glass. Green, blue, red, yellow, and amber shards, catching the sunlight. I lay in the sun until the tide touched my shoes; then I crawled around on my knees, combing around for the luminescent green pieces.

I didn't look up and bumped into an older woman who was filling a leather pouch with shards.

"I like the green ones too," she said. "They're real neon. Nineteenth-century Vaseline bottles. They glow if you put them under black light."

She took me around on my hands and knees and explained where all the colors came from. Amber: aromatherapy bottles. White: milk bottles. She told me red was very rare, as were black and turquoise. Her favorite color—which was also the hardest to find—was amethyst. She told me her name was Venus and that she was from Rancho Cucamonga. I told her my name was Grace.

"That's my favorite name," she said. "It's my son's name. I know, a little weird. I just liked it. I don't like rules so much."

As usual, I wondered if it was a sign; the messenger of self-acceptance, shooting arbitrary arrows of meaning into my life.

Afterward I walked to a cliff with the goal of sitting still for a few hours. I wanted to keep my eyes closed, focus on sensations, land back in my body. I let all the sounds wash over me and imagined I could hear every single thing happening anywhere: the wind; mountains growing; every car horn in every city; people talking and whispering; drilling, exploding, melting. The world coming together and wrapping me up in a textured hum.

Early the next day I drove back to Los Angeles. At a gas station in the Valley someone in a suit and no shoes approached me. They asked my name.

"Grace. What about you?"

"I don't know!" they said angrily. Then they turned and sprinted away.

4

Soon after anna left, my sister's chronic illness grew unmanageable again. In recent years, she'd gotten continually sicker as invasive uterine tissue spread throughout her abdomen, strangling her other organs, even into her legs and back. The part of me that believes the universe is governed by an unscientific but moral law of consequence feared that her ailments were conspiratorial: stop reproducing yourself, I worried her body was saying.

After a few months of not seeing her—this was regular for us, even when we were in the same city—I drove across town to pick her up from a lunch meeting and bring her back to my house. She stepped outside the restaurant with a woman I recognized from an early 2000s sitcom. The woman appeared not to notice that my sister, however effusive she was, had a film of dissociation over her eyes.

When we got in the car, she dissolved into her pain. I pushed the passenger seat back so she could lie horizontal and bring her legs up to her chest. She squeezed her eyes shut, started breathing fast and shallow, a pain-management tool she'd been taught by one of dozens of care providers whom I'd tried to keep track of, all with different credentials, areas of expertise, and beliefs.

She'd never seen where I lived, an orange and blue house I shared with Lake and a tawny, knee-height dog who looks like a fawn. When I first moved in I was worried I was going to fall in love with Lake. She treated making a pot of tea like an event and used the garage to make drawings of feminine entities with ropes growing where their genitals should be. A month into living with her, I said, "I have a crush on you."

"Just...don't," she replied.

We've eaten most meals together since, falling asleep in her bed with the dog between us on nights when the house was cold or either of us was lonely.

Inviting my sister over was an attempt to break a cycle of mutual hurt. I said our relationship only consisted of me entering the spaces of her life; she rebutted that I never welcomed her into mine. Our disagreements always became tautologies.

In anticipation of lunch, I'd imagined driving her to the

neighborhood I lived in and pointing things out to her along the way: Elysian Park, where the city demolished the neighborhoods in Chavez Ravine so they could build Dodger Stadium; the abandoned Lincoln Heights Jail on Avenue 19, where they locked up cross-dressers in the 1950s; the LA River, a trickle of water in an angular flume of concrete. I wanted to pull her into my worldview so that we could find shared meaning, even briefly.

I wanted her to meet Lake, the dog, drink tea with us, see the way we lived. *This is my life,* I thought. *I'm proud of it.* Maybe some part of me wanted her to envy it, too.

She had clearly summoned all her available energy to get through lunch. She kept panting, half-asleep, while I drove. I abandoned my planned tour and drove home by the quickest route, trying to avoid bumps so the car wouldn't shake her insides and make her body hurt more than it already did.

During the drive, two of her doctors called; she couldn't speak beyond a mumble, so I held the phone and talked to both of them, relaying what she had told me before she'd become incoherent—acute, numbing pain in her lower back and right leg; heavy bleeding; insurmountable nausea.

The first doctor said he'd called in two painkillers, neither of which I could pronounce, to the Walgreens nearest my house. The second doctor said she needed to go in for surgery the next day. A removal of tissue, a scraping of her insides, a shift to the left or right of an organ. With the help of the unpronounceable painkillers, she'd make her way through the remainder of Sunday. At this point, being cut open and entered was a regular occurrence for her. The prospect of surgery seemed to calm her down. Relief at the possibility that something, anything, would make being in her body more bearable.

It was not lost on me that my reproductive system functioned seamlessly, despite my having no use for it.

Sisterhood makes it difficult to distinguish between bodies. At least, as the one born six years later, I've found it nearly impossible not to experience her sorrow as my own. It sits in my chest, heavy and constant. If she is lonely, I am lonely. If she is afraid, I feel it too. The desire to protect her from pain is not an altruistic one. It's to protect myself, too. The only other option would be to carve her out of my chest altogether, which I could never, and would never, do.

When she first got famous I had a nightmare in which I wore her skin like an outfit and attended an event in her place. The dream ended with a mob of people ripping the skin off of me in strips. The skin had fused onto me, adhered to my nerve endings, and become my own, so that when they ripped it off there was pink, sinewy muscle underneath, my heartbeat visibly pumping through the veins. I crouched on the ground until I was fully skinned, just pink, twitching muscle. The pain was worse than anything I'd felt in my waking life.

Outside my house, I helped her out of the car and to the door. I had cleaned to prepare for her visit—mopped the kitchen and bathroom floors, vacuumed all the corners,

folded blankets, fluffed pillows, organized books and news-
papers. I wanted her to know I could keep a home. But she
was in a daze, so I led her up to my room, where I tucked her
into my bed and gave her a heavy blue rock to hold in her
hand. I thought that holding something cold and solid would
ground her enough to keep the pain from carrying her away.
I opened the screen door so the breeze could come in.

"I like all the bird sounds," she said. "It's cozy."

She drifted in and out of sleep while I read beside her. I
made her tea and peeled an orange I'd taken from a neighbor's tree. I'd memorized which houses had which fruit
in which season; guavas in early fall, persimmons in late
autumn and winter, citrus in spring. I'd found date palms
and pomegranates, and green tomato vines growing out of
a trash-covered hillside.

I put the orange and tea next to her on a tray while she
slept. She mumbled, breathed deeply, but didn't wake up.
When we were kids we slept together in a lofted bed that
looked out over the air shaft in the back of the building,
a cavernous chute with no doors leading to it, decades of
dust at the bottom. The air shaft made a strange humming
sound. I couldn't sleep facing it because I was convinced
someone was trapped alone at the bottom. I was afraid
either she or I would get sucked down there, be trapped
forever. I'd lie awake in the middle of the night, eyes wide
in the dark, on guard, protecting us both from the air
shaft's pull.

Now, seeing her sleep in my space, among my few but

precious possessions, I felt I had the infrastructure to take care of her, to be a respite from her chaos, a protector. With my own structure in place, I could hold her pain, rather than getting swept away by it. And, perhaps, if the structure were stable enough to contain her, it might also contain me. Neither one of us would get taken away.

Half-awake, she talked about how she hadn't felt safe in months. I told her to stay for a few days, unsure whether she could hear me. I'll make you more tea, I said, soup, and solid food when you get hungry.

"I love you," she said, four times.

I remember her as a little girl, tortured by fours and eights. She had to do everything four or eight times, like say "I love you, good night," or turn the light switch on and off, or stop and turn in circles on cracks in the sidewalk. One night my parents had to carry her through the house crying and screaming because she thought if she didn't keep counting she'd get AIDS. When I needed to cry, I was so ashamed that I went and hid in the closet, held my breath so I wouldn't make any sounds.

When she stopped being able to control the numbers at all, she had to start taking a medication that made her tired all the time and made her sweat in the night. We shared a bed because we were both too scared to sleep alone. I tried to sleep as close to the edge as I could, so the sweat wouldn't get to me. She got chubby and couldn't do her homework. I was humiliated by her, for failing to be a regular girl. Her failure entered my body, like I was failing, too.

I never told my parents or her that eight was my number, too. The number I needed to get to when I counted items of clothing on men's bodies or cycled through visions of girls and women. I didn't want my family to think I was crazy also. I pushed the eight down below language, where it was real without being a part of my persona. I can't remember if I took eight from her or if we came to it independently, because of its balance.

She slept through the afternoon; I came and went from my bedroom, doing chores. I knew my desire to hold her hostage in my house, in my life, was born out of my resistance to hers. But I was also stubborn in my certainty that I, of anyone in her life, was in the best position to let her rest, to let her disappear.

I wanted to show her the small acts that grounded me each day: make a pot of coffee, do the dishes, sweep the kitchen floor, water the plants. Moments that are for no one, toward nothing, except the maintenance of a day. Moments not worth being written about, maybe, but that make me feel the most connected to being alive.

I found myself fantasizing about a future in which she would take care of a garden, walk her dog, fry an egg and put it on toast, take pleasure in scrubbing the bathtub clean. She would have eight books by her bed, or eight vases on the windowsill. Eight isn't evil anymore in this fantasy. It is hers now, and it protects her. If I visualize this clearly enough, maybe she'll accept what I'm trying to offer her: the space to be quiet and the pleasure of being invisible.

*   *   *

I'd been hurt by my sister sketching me in her work with the broad strokes required to create a character. The character got inside me, disoriented me. The power of the page is such that I couldn't tell what was real, her story or my own. I splintered into multiple truths until my own recollection seemed like nothing more than an abstraction. Is there any way to write about the people who shape my life without reenacting the flattening that's been done to me? Writing about someone I love, someone toward whom my love is pained and tangled, I feel I've failed before I started.

Taking my own life as subject matter makes me feel like a woman. There's no theoretical praxis for this. It's an emotion more than a belief. The most rigorous analysis I have is that everything in my life—who I am, what I do, what I don't do—exists in an unbreakable duality with my sister. She, the woman. She, the writer. There are only two options: to be her or reject her.

I don't have the language for why I equate womanhood with subjecthood. It's an equation I was given at a young age. Woman tells her story. Man listens. In all her gendered glory, I saw and continue to see my sister as having incalculable agency, indomitable power. This is precisely why I revere her. This is precisely why I am able to be angry at her.

After my sister's surgery, I spent two nights with her in her hospital room. I tried to sleep under a starchy white sheet, on a couch my legs hung off of. The nurses came in at hourly intervals to check her vitals. The lights were never fully off. I wrapped the stiff fabric around me in a cocoon, lay on my back, and used the mechanical hum of the building to lull me into a half-awake trance. She woke up hungry, and I went down to the cafeteria to get plain pasta, a roll with butter, or a white bread and cheese sandwich.

The next night, after my sister fell asleep, I left the hospital to meet my friend stella (who, unlike the other Stella, chooses to spell her name with a lowercase *s*). When I'd first met stella, she was visiting town and staying in the home of her friend's father. I drove to pick her up and the home turned out to be a French provincial mansion behind a gate at the top of Mulholland Drive. I rang the buzzer and a famous American actor opened the door in a striped pajama suit, not unlike the one my father wears. Not unlike the one I wear, actually.

"Do you like my house?" he asked.

He led me to the breakfast table, where he was doing a crossword puzzle and eating curried chicken for breakfast.

"Are you an actress?" he asked. "You have star power."

He'd caught the stench of fame on me, I guess.

I met stella at a bar in Hollywood, twenty minutes east of the hospital. We had two drinks each; then I said I had to leave, to get back to my sister.

"If you saw yourself as separate from her," stella said, "you might finally feel free."

I returned to the hospital with even greater determination

to care for my sister. I also knew that in the middle of the night, softened by IV painkillers and antianxiety medication, she would confide in me that she was unhappy. I wanted to hear her say it wasn't just her illness. I wanted to hear her say it was her life. I sat in a hospital chair, a foot from her bed, listened to her lamentations, and fulfilled my own confirmation biases. Proof: that fame was what was harming her; that we were still connected enough to see the same things; that this period of her life might end up having been a brief experiment.

If I felt compelled to protect her, then I might have reason not to blame her. It wasn't her fault. It wasn't her fault. It wasn't her fault. It wasn't her fault. She was just a little girl, swallowed up by a big bad machine. And I was her sister, her dutiful sister. Two daughters. Works of art.

When I imagined myself a decade into the future, I saw something in the shape of a man, tall but lean, soft stubble on his face but hair nowhere else on his body. But the word "sister" hovered over him, neon, glowing. It felt more indelible than my own name, my own body. I don't know why. I told myself it was because she was famous, because the fact of our sisterhood had been dragged into public without my consent; in fact, sisterhood had always dominated my sense of self, for as long as I'd been conscious.

Seeing her as a victim of her own opportunity was the best way to keep the myth alive. What myth? The myth that our family was special. The myth that we were biologically linked for a reason. The myth that as the children of artists we had inherited their greatness and were carrying it forward. The myth that we deserved what we had. The myth that the lives of people who make things are more significant than everyone else's.

These myths were all one and the same to me.

The substance of fame wasn't something I'd only seen touching and changing others. It had changed me. It made me paranoid, on edge in every interaction, wondering whether people knew I was connected to fame, were triggered by it, and so saw me as a walking trigger. I saw myself as a physical embodiment of a hierarchy in which some people's lives are considered more valuable than others, and as a corrective for that violence, I wanted to disappear entirely.

When I looked at her, I saw a character transported to a hospital bed, a pixelated billboard momentarily captured in human form. When she was sick, at least, I could remember she was mortal. Her sleeping form brought continuity, drew a line back in time from now to the air shaft we slept next to as children, the cavern by our bed that threatened to swallow us up.

Our father came to Los Angeles. Whatever was inside me— a propensity for incurable isolation—I knew, on some level, I'd gotten from him. Being a father had given him purpose, had eased the emptiness. I suspected he'd be happy if we went back to him, moved into our childhood bedrooms, let him make us toast every morning. And sometimes I wanted to, though I knew I couldn't.

When I was little, I ran away when my dad tried to pick me up or hug me. I turned my head away so that he couldn't kiss my cheek. I hated the hair on his arms and the stubble on his face. I knew I hurt his feelings, but the more hurt he felt, the more I didn't want to be near him. Once he leaned down to pick me up and I threw a basketball at him and shattered his glasses. Another time I punched him in the nose. Looking at him filled me with rage. I knew he was a good dad, but I couldn't help the angry feeling.

He used to tell my sister and me that women were superior to men. Being female was divine, he said; it was something to be proud of. He even said sometimes that he wished he was a woman, because women understood what was happening around them more than men did, because women got to talk about their feelings and be soft with one another. When he was a kid in the fifties, his favorite show was *American Bandstand* and he'd stand in front of the TV and slow dance with the air.

My sister had moved to a hotel room on the Sunset Strip for the remainder of her recovery. I sat in an armchair, using my laptop as a shield, observing my father compulsively adjust the lighting, try to open the sealed-shut windows, and demand that she drink water, which she had never enjoyed doing. She protested while also appearing to take comfort in his orders. Father and daughter—their dynamic was well rehearsed and swiftly returned to. His attempts to manage chaos had repulsed me since I was a child. His fury at a departure time two minutes later than expected. His panic at a light turned too bright. His horror at a towel left on the floor instead of draped over a hook. Few things seemed more male than this assertion of power through arbitrary administration. As I aged, I noticed the same inclinations in myself. The more aware I became of our similarities, the more I began to regard him with an aching tenderness.

When my father or sister referred to me using "she" pronouns, they stuck in me like tiny hooks. Not that I had invited them to do otherwise. But still, I kept track of how many times they each said "she," and the number hung above our interactions, proof of my delusion. The more times they said "she," the more convinced I was that "she" would always be me. Quantity held validity. She. She. She. She. I couldn't bring myself to ask my dad not to call me "girlie." It was just a word. I could defend anyone else's right to gendered self-determination, but I couldn't take the girlie away from him.

After my sister fell asleep, I watched her face contort with pain. Her nose crinkled and her eyes twitched. She'd never stopped being a little girl. She was just a little body, full of fear and dreams. I wanted her to be safe and out of pain. I wanted her to have a different body more than I wanted myself to. It was a flicker of a feeling and soon it was washed away by panic, as the room closed in on me.

I couldn't stay. If I stayed I'd lose myself.

5

A FEW WEEKS AFTER leaving my sister, I got a cryptic text from my mother: "Can you do me a favor?"

It was one a.m. in California and four a.m. in the Northeast. I was at a house in the far north San Fernando Valley, in pseudo-ranch country, that friends had rented on Airbnb for a birthday party. There was a stable at the end of the street, and large watercolors of white men on horseback and vintage wagon wheels hung in the house's hallways. We found secret bookcases in the office full of blue and red leather-bound volumes of advanced Scientological language and protocol. Some of us sprawled across the carpeted floor to read entries from dictionaries and excerpts from an "auditor's guide" aloud to one another.

"If there is a process which one should do with another process," I read, "then that process should be understood thoroughly, for if done incorrectly it would be likely to produce confusion into all the other processes...therefore, let us examine with rigor the name of this process. It is the REMEDY OF HAVINGNESS."

It didn't seem so off base. Systems thinking: all processes affect other processes; nothing exists without anything else.

"This is profound," I said.

"Do not start with that," someone said.

I usually felt conspicuous in the relative likelihood of my joining a community ruled by dogma, even if it was Scientology, just to be a part of something. Just to remedy my lack of havingness.

Alas, later in the manual: "By 'remedy' one means the correction of any aberrated condition. By 'havingness' one means mass or objects. It means the remedy of a preclear's native ability to acquire things at will and reject them at will."

I'd migrated to the bathroom when my mother texted me. A group of people were piled into the lukewarm whirl-pool bathtub, eating wet chocolate cake.

"?," I texted.

"Will you bring me a puppy? She's an Old-Time Scotch Collie. She's in the desert outside LA."

In May, after my time in the hospital with my sister, I

buried myself in writing the story of Zoya. I needed this after losing track of myself during the interlude with my sister and father. If the two poles of existence were dedication to family and dedication to the romantic, it was safer to choose the latter. At least my life would have a trajectory of differentiation: from loyal daughter-sister to lover. As a lover, I could be a boy.

But I could not resist the opportunity to be of service to my mother. As a child, I went almost everywhere with her, no matter what she had to do. Shopping, to the doctor, to work, to meetings, to parties, to see friends, to the bank, to the post office. At stores I sat in the changing room and watched her try things on, giving my opinion. After school, she gave me the job of answering the phone in her studio, which was two floors below our fourth-floor apartment, in a former button factory. Back then she had long red hair that she dyed with henna in the bathtub. I helped her coat her wet hair with hot paste, which made the water run green. Her hair had five colors in it: red, purple, gold, pink, and silver at the roots when she didn't dye it for a few weeks. Her nails were usually red too. I sat beside her while her manicures dried, keeping her company. When I was young and she got sad, I tried to be helpful and mature, so that she'd feel better. Her sadness was usually because of something having to do with art, like when she felt excluded from something, or overlooked. She said she felt "invisible." This seemed odd because, to me, she was more visible, more important, than anything or anyone else.

She explained that feeling invisible wasn't rational. It's just something you *feel*. That you can't explain away.

The assignment of bringing her a dog, then, a creature in which she could invest unbounded care, had particular significance. My mother reserves her purest sweetness for children and dogs.

The ashes of our childhood dog, Dean—for James Dean—still sat in a box in the corner of the living room. Dean was a wirehaired fox terrier, like Asta from *The Thin Man*. I'd been urging her to get another dog since Dean's passing.

She had grown up with collies—first Cindy, then Torney—living props in the perfect set that was her 1950s Jewish suburban childhood. She told me stories about Cindy when I was young and couldn't sleep. Cindy escaping and coming back three days later covered in nettles and mud. Cindy falling into the garbage chute. Cindy eating her father's cigars. Cindy, our very own Lassie.

I imagined myself showing up at my parents' door, basketball-sized collie puppy in my arms, wrapped in a bow. In the fantasy, I was taller, more muscular, flat-chested; broad shoulders and harder, rougher skin; overgrown hair brushed to the side. Handsome and stern, but with smiling eyes. Dutifully at my parents' doorstep, the puppy in my lithe arms, I would be the messenger of my mother's joy.

I texted her back within five minutes and told her I would get the dog.

"I'm going to name her Penny," she said. "Do you like it?"

"It's perfect," I said.

* * *

Two days later, I drove into the desert east of Los Angeles to collect Penny from her breeder's house. Breeder. The word mortified me. Likely for its connotation with the genre of porn—that is, "Mean stepfather breeds stepson who is late for curfew" or "Muscle daddy breeds innocent twink"—I watched when I was too anxious or depressed to do anything else. I didn't even watch it to get off, just to be calmed by the manifested and rhythmic need of the top, and the docile willingness of the bottom.

When sex became part of my life, at the end of adolescence, my "vagina" evoked nothing. It was a non-part. When others touched me, I floated up and away from the scene, imitating the arousal I'd watched them experience. Being touched tickled at best, stung at worst. But, false as my responses were, the performance of pleasure seemed to satisfy my partners.

On my own, the only way I liked to touch myself was to insert things inside my asshole. When I started allowing other people to touch me this way too, I came with another person for the first time. It was the only experience I'd ever had of my body overcoming me, instead of the other way around. Getting fucked in the ass rendered me a boy for its duration. Afterward, I had to make do again with the reality of my anatomy.

It started with my parents teaching me how to wipe. First, you took the toilet paper, folded it into a square, and wiped yourself. For the front, you used two squares folded into one. For the back, you used as many as possible, folded up into a wad. It was hard to feel clean after. If I stained my underwear, I wadded them up in a ball and hid them under my bed or in the closet. I went in my underwear once while a babysitter was taking care of me. She had freckles and wore spaghetti-strap tank tops and was from Maine. I stuck the underwear behind the dresser in the bathroom. A couple of hours later, she came out of the bathroom and said she knew what I'd done.

After that, I decided I wouldn't go anymore. It was too disgusting. I hated what came out of me. When I felt it coming I just tightened up and stayed still until the feeling went away. The longer I didn't go, the scarier the thought of going became. It would hurt too much.

I got stomachaches that made me fall on the floor crying. I stopped eating because my body was already full of food. My parents called a therapist, then asked me gentle questions like "Are you afraid to give up control?" and "Did something scary happen in a bathroom?" The questions didn't help. I got so sick that they brought me to a doctor. The nurses and my parents held me down while the doctor put something called an enema inside me, which shot warm water up into my body. It was a scary, wet feeling that I hated, until the water came out, which tickled and relaxed me even though it made me cry.

After the doctors held me down, I started putting my fingers and other things inside myself when I was alone.

Different holes felt different ways. My body was like the shell of a hermit crab sometimes, or like the armor at the Metropolitan Museum. Putting my fingers inside myself felt like reaching inside the shell. I touched the part of myself that was warm and liquid.

The year after I wouldn't go to the bathroom, I started refusing to sleep. I worried that if I let myself sleep I wouldn't come back. No matter how tired I was, I kept my eyes open and stared straight ahead in the dark. Once my parents fell asleep, I tiptoed to their bedroom and stood outside the door. Sometimes I got dizzy and nauseous from how tired I was, but I didn't give in.

During the day I stored up bad thoughts that I could flip through at night to keep me awake: people being killed by lava in Pompeii; people being buried alive; people waking up on the morning of their own execution; prisoners of war being tortured in dungeons; children being kept in basements by men. Everything terrible that had ever happened filled the dark, wrapping me up. Putting my fingers inside myself was the only way to calm down, to be in my body instead of lost in the chaos of the whole world.

On the way east to get Penny, I stopped at a pet store in a mall to buy her the red collar and leash my mother had requested. I also browsed for metal ones, running my fingers over the spiked loops. Not for Penny; I had someone else in mind.

"How do you put this on?" I asked a sweaty clerk.

"Well, how big is your dog?"

"Big. A big mutt. Um, sort of a hound. Big but with a medium neck." I held my hands at my hips to show the imaginary dog's height.

"It's better if you bring your dog in to try it on."

"He doesn't live here."

. I bought the largest size and packed it in my duffel bag, separate from the tote I filled with Penny's future possessions.

The breeder lived at the end of a dirt road, in a low house encircled by a chain-link fence, dividing its parcel of sand from the rest of the desert. Her compound was the last before undeveloped land, prickly Joshua trees quivering for miles, big, tan rocks at the horizon.

The door of the house opened and two tall collies bolted out, galloping toward me. The breeder followed, her long brown hair parted in the middle. She looked like a 1960s folk singer.

"Hiya," she said. She talked like one, too.

Inside, six bouncing collie puppies swarmed me in unison. They shook and pranced, vibrating.

"Which one is Penny?"

She reached down for the one with the shortest nose.

"Hey, Cinnamon! Off! Off, Cinnamon!" She flicked a tawnier one off Penny and handed her to me, a squirming ball.

"You should know," she said, "that Penny may not be very comfortable around men. My friends come around sometimes, but I'm not friends with any men."

"You really think she can tell?"

"Oh yeah."

She wriggled around in my arms while I tried to hold her, flopped onto the linoleum floor, and slipped over to her siblings. I worried the breeder would be able to tell Penny didn't trust me and would refuse to let her drive back to Los Angeles with me.

On the drive out to the desert, a child at a bathroom rest stop in Chino had asked me what I was doing in the women's restroom. I'd thought for a second before saying, "I'm female." The qualifier had slipped out, despite the fact that its premise was one I claimed not to believe in.

"Oh," the child had said. She looked me up and down, unconvinced, and ran after her mother.

I sat down in a leather easy chair and the breeder put Penny back on my lap. She jumped off and ran up to her own mother, a tall, sylphlike creature with the grace of a unicorn. Penny hurled herself at her mother's legs until her mother lay down on the ground beside her, so that Penny could curl up in the curve of her hind legs and stomach.

"Will she be okay without her mom?" I asked the breeder.

"Oh yeah, she'll adjust."

"But how hard will it be at first? Will she cry?"

"You can take a towel with her mom's scent on it, if you're worried."

At the peak of my childhood sleep phobia, I slept with my face buried in one of my mother's cashmere sweaters. The fabric smelled of Féminité du Bois, the discontinued

Shiseido perfume she'd worn my whole life. She hoarded boxes of it under the bathroom sink. A scent- and texture-based pacifier, it made lying awake in the dark, engulfed in a cloud of the world's most violent potentials, more bearable. At that time, I told her every day that I never wanted to stop living with her.

"You'll be ready when the time comes," she said.

Though I hadn't believed it then, her prediction had turned out to be true. The space of childhood could no longer contain me, as much as I wished I could fit inside it. It had been one thing to exist inside the world my parents had created for me when I was a teenager and my sexuality lurked under the surface. Now my transgressions were too real to be pushed down.

Penny, though: she was still too young to be ripped away from her mother. Unless she contained some desire I couldn't see, the kind that made her unsuitable for daughterhood.

Outside, the breeder handed Penny to me, wrapped in her mother-scented towel. As we drove away down the dirt road, Penny kept her gaze fixed on the back window, staring at her former home receding into the distance. Long strands of viscous drool leaked from her panting mouth. I reached over and used the mother-scented cloth to soak the spit up. She whimpered. It looked like her eyes were filling with tears.

"It's gonna be okay, sweet girl. I promise. It's gonna be okay."

My mother, intent on Penny's safe delivery, purchased

me an economy-plus plane ticket, so that Penny could stay crated at my feet, rather than having to fly in the cargo hold. But she spent the plane ride in my lap, intermittently staring into my eyes and inserting her long nose into my water cup. I didn't read, watch a movie, even nap; instead, I spent the five hours petting her head, kissing the soft red hair over her eyes, a foot soldier of my mother's love. The journey reminded me of a recurring dream I had in which I held my young self in my arms. At some point in the dream, I put young Grace down and followed her along an amalgamation of different streets, past willow trees, neoclassical buildings, a schoolhouse, a court building. I walked slightly behind, studying her sturdy walk, her hands swinging at her sides.

Penny and I landed in Hartford and my parents met us by baggage claim. I saw my mother from a distance, a bowl of water and a bag of treats in her hands. I had already dressed Penny in her red collar.

"I love you, Penny," she said, holding her in her arms. "I know you had a long journey to get here, but I love you so much already." The way she spoke to the dog was so familiar: soft encouragement and unconditionality, the way she'd spoken to me when I was a little girl.

I may have given the impression that I was devout in my commitment to Zoya and, as a result, celibate. Actually, I'd fallen in love with someone a month earlier.

Joshua had come to LA to visit Rex, a best friend who was staying with me while Lake was traveling for the month. Rex and I entered a kind of cohabitating symbiosis: we slept, ate, and bathed together; she encouraged me to redirect all the energy I'd been sending toward other people—Zoya, Antonia, my family—toward myself.

Rex had told me a year earlier that if I met Joshua, another best friend of hers, I'd fall in love with them. Joshua was beautiful—long red hair, blue eyes, pale skin—and this made me feign disinterest in them.

"I don't think I'd like them," I told Rex.

"You're wrong," she said. "Don't be fooled by their container. They're an alien."

Coming from Rex, this was the highest compliment.

Joshua and Rex both ended up staying with me. Joshua was disarmingly kind, seemingly without expectations that their gestures of care and consideration would be returned. I went out for the day and came back to a house full of flowers or formerly ripped shirts repaired and folded neatly on my bed. They made themself breakfast and left me some too, the food divided into quadrants according to color, a cloth draped over the bowl to keep it warm. It's not that I hadn't been cared for before, but that the care I was used to receiving implicitly carried with it an understanding that it was a privilege to receive it, that it might be revoked if it wasn't met with adequate gratitude. I can't say whether this expectation was communicated in the care itself, or if my conditioning made me project scarcity. It has always been an honor to receive anything, anything at all, from a "woman." In the receiving, I felt real.

Joshua seemed honored to give. This was not the kind of woman with whom I was familiar. It quickly became clear that Joshua was not a woman at all.

We went to the beach one day and I buried them in sand. A man walked by and told them they looked like a beautiful mermaid. Disappointment flickered in their eyes, and I recognized their dissociation. They transmuted in front of my eyes into an alien that had been consigned to an imitation of beauty, beauty that looked like womanhood. They were a translucent creature, full of spit and organs, orange-colored fur growing out of their pores in a long mane from skull to hips. It was absurd they'd ever been misrecognized as anything else. That absurdity had levity. It made me feel hopeful, less fixed.

Walking back up the dunes from the beach, I asked them if they were a girl.

"Oh," they said. "Thank you for asking." Their grin communicated how deeply the answer was no, how much of an impossibility yes was.

The last night they were in town we stayed up late, talking. I told them about Zoya and they told me it sounded like loving her gave me structure.

"She's your invisible dog collar," they said.

We turned the lights off and held each other in the dark. Soon we were rubbing against each other. I gyrated with a clumsy fervor that defied all my rules of composure and control. We squirmed around, worms in dirt, until we were a clump, and we came, and we were worms in repose.

They left Los Angeles the next day and I found a letter under my pillow, written in red ink. "I'll get you a real collar," it said. "I'll take you on long walks, and if you ask nicely, I'll let you walk around by yourself, too."

Later that week, they sent me a stainless steel collar in the mail. A bone-shaped tag hung from it, engraved with the words "Good Boy."

So, after leaving Penny with my parents, I took the train to Joshua's Chinatown apartment, the metal choke collar and dog tag in my duffel bag, amused and creeped out by a narrative coherence. Delivering a dog to my mother, then delivering myself to my new owner.

They led me to their bed, a piece of yellow foam they'd cut in two and stacked on top of itself. Their cats, a tabby and a calico, slept curled up in piles of clothing on the floor. They ordered me to go get my collar. I dug through my duffel, handed it to them, and then got on my hands and knees while they clasped it around my neck. They clipped on a leash. They slowly, carefully, submerged their entire hand inside me. Then, slowly, the other. At first, I watched myself fill up from the outside. But as they addressed me directly—good boy, good boy, good boy, good boy—I was pulled into presence. Full from deep inside myself, barred from escape.

Afterward, I lay on the yellow foam, crying. The nice thing about being a dog was that it was okay to feel pathetic. It was okay to need your owner, to let them control you. Show up, eager and open, willing to love and be loved. Derive purpose from making one's owner proud. The same life every day. And it was much less sinister than being a boy.

At first the healing swell of new love kept my depression at bay. But by the middle of summer, I couldn't get out of bed. Either my medication stopped working or my depression became too unwieldy for the meds to contain it; either way, my desire to disappear crossed over into a suspicion that it was best not to be alive. I went home to hide in my parents' house while I "cross-titrated" off one antidepressant and onto another.

If language fails me here it is because language fails me here. If I sound clinical it is because it is easier to be clinical. Writing is inherently optimistic for me. A leap of faith that, if I try to communicate, I will be understood. So for me one of the main symptoms of depression, of hopelessness, of total, all-encompassing cynicism, is to lose my belief in writing and to stop being able to leap. Why describe something when I'll never be understood? Why not simply rely on the definitions and diagnoses provided by the American Psychiatric Association's *Diagnostic and Statistical Manual of Mental Disorders*?

F64.1: Gender Dysphoria in Adolescents and Adults
F41.1: Generalized Anxiety Disorder
F50.89: Avoidant/Restrictive Food Intake Disorder
F42.2: Obsessive-Compulsive Disorder

Yes, that's me. Here I am. I am F64.1, F41.1, F50.89, F42.2. I am full of Fs and 4s and .s. I have a 6, a 5, an 8, a 9. I have two 2s. If you understand me, what I'm called, will I stop feeling like a body suspended alone in some part of the universe without any other floating matter, astral bodies, specks of light on the horizon? It's either metaphors or numerical codes. At least the latter is less dramatic.

When I was able to get out of bed, I helped my parents cook and pick and wash vegetables from their garden, or watched British serial crime shows with them. There was a comfort in adolescent regression. Feeling trapped was the closest I knew to being held. The only thing I looked forward to doing was walking Penny, who was now twice the size she'd been when I first picked her up in the desert.

Much of my day revolved around Penny's cycle of needs. I took her around the perimeter of the yard, so she could grow familiar with the boundaries of her existence. I picked her up and carried her over the boundary, so she could only conceive of leaving if escorted.

In the mornings, I sat outside and watched Penny wander around the yard. She never went so far that she lost sight of me. Sometimes I caught her eating whole hydrangeas off a bush. The petals stuck to her lips and eyelashes like snow. She liked to sit under trees and watch leaves fall slowly, side to side. Her body stayed still but her eyes darted back and forth. Every few minutes I'd beckon her over, just to watch her barrel toward me and crouch at my feet.

"Watch me, Penny! Watch me!" This was the primary

command my mother opted for instead of "Come." It demanded a moment of eye contact before further direction.

A few times my mother accidentally yelled, "Watch me, Grace! Watch me!" or called me Penny in the kitchen, when I was making coffee, then giggled at her mistake.

"Freudian, huh?"

In August, I let Joshua come to my parents' house to keep me company. I feared letting someone see me so weak. I worried they were finding purpose in the job of loving me. But I'd done that with others so many times before. What right did I have to reject it?

"It's okay to need me," they insisted.

My parents' home was a dollhouse. Perfectly placed black-and-white candelabras and strange sculptures that mimicked the swirls and curls in the wallpaper. Victorian fancy meets gothic haunting meets art deco fourth dimension. I wandered through the house like I was tripping, elements of the decor becoming animated, the art on the walls announcing its needs, its judgments, its will. I couldn't walk through the second-floor staircase vestibule without all the German expressionist graphite pencil drawings smothering me in their preconfiguration of the Nazi agenda. Who were these naked women with party-hat-shaped breasts who had been reproduced by men in rimless glasses, like my own? Were the girls sixteen, seventeen, eighteen? Were they lovers or models for hire? Were they sex workers? Were they Jewish? Had the painters fucked them?

My dissociation made the house so grotesque that I

observed its inhabitants like an anthropologist. In the living room, in a glass cabinet, evidence of the homeowners' children—clay sculptures, stick-figure drawings of a family, cardboard dioramas, framed, printed photographs of two little white girls in matching red one-piece bathing suits. One of the children, Grace, had made dozens of clay busts of men, with square jaws and mustaches that curled up around their lips. Some of the busts were covered in phallic protrusions on their faces, chests, scalps, and arms. Some of the sculptures even looked like giant phalluses, giving birth to dozens of mini phalluses, covered in even littler phalluses. Phallus trees, masked as abstraction. What an *odd* little girl. Little pervert.

Sometimes Joshua and I took Penny on quiet walks, or we worked on teaching her to roll over and lift her paw. Joshua read or drew in bed next to me while I half slept and half cried. I didn't know if or why I was sad. It seemed eternal. Years of grief—for what, I didn't know—surfacing for a purge.

Joshua was patient with my incapacity. It wasn't urgent to them that I "feel better." They seemed to believe that whatever I was going through was necessary.

"Caterpillars don't turn directly into butterflies," they said. "They make a cocoon so that they can turn into goo, and then re-form."

Joshua relied on the natural world for metaphors and seemed to have an unending store of them. It was part of their bodilyness, part of how they kept me close to earth and also why they made me squirm. Dirt, shit, grass, rot, cum, sweat, drool, and mold. Whereas I was appalled by any proof of my own materiality, mortality, they were soothed by it. They didn't see the difference between themself and organic matter.

Goo, they kept saying. You're in your goo stage.

I had lived under the illusion, my entire life, that within the chrysalis the caterpillar's body simply stretched, shrank, and molted into a butterfly. I asked Joshua to read me encyclopedia entries explaining the process and learned that the caterpillar actually enters the chrysalis in order to eat itself alive. In that digestion, it becomes like a soup, liquid life that will ooze out of the cocoon if you slice it in half. When I learned the term "self-determination" I imagined it involved an act of miraculous creation. But the caterpillar destroys itself to determine itself. The killing and the becoming are one and the same. Out of its eating itself, its utter decomposition, it is born.

6

I GREW UP THINKING that the saddest thing possible was to die a nobody. I remember lying in bed awake at night, haunted by all the people I'd passed on the street that day whom no one would remember. How many years after their death until it was as if they had never existed at all? I remember feeling smothered on skinny streets with tall buildings on either side, wondering how many people alone in their apartments were loved by no one. I thought about all the people in the world alone in cages and rooms with no windows, hidden away. It seemed to me that if you were on no one's mind, you were as good as dead. The greatest punishment possible was being forgotten.

When I was little, I thought I'd be famous when I grew up. At the very least, I would be *great*. It seemed like the only possible conclusion. That's what happened to special people. And I had been told, again and again, that I was one of the most special of all. I had a special family and I lived in a special world. Everyone in it would, should, be remembered.

By the time I was a teenager I knew it was unseemly to admit my belief in my own value out loud. I still believed it, though. I clung to it. When I had disgusting thoughts, desires, I recited mantras to myself, affirming my own superiority. *I'm special. I'm great. I will be greater than them.*

When my sister got famous, I was terrified. It had happened to her, and this was when it occurred to me that it might not happen to me. The only thing that seemed worse than being a nobody was wishing for greatness and not getting it.

I dealt with this pain by trying to eat alive the part of me that had always believed I'd get what she'd already gotten. Preeminent known-ness. And I ate it alive by deciding it was evil. By deciding that fame was the counterpoint and, as such, the sibling of the processes that locked people away in rooms so they'd be forgotten. If I told myself success was evil, if I really believed it, then maybe I wouldn't want it anymore.

Whenever I noticed the desire in myself to be praised, to be recognized or rewarded, I told myself I was awful.

I became a stand-in for the monolithic violence that made some people demigods and some people subhuman.

Analyzing the ideological violence of your own fear and longing is not, I've learned, the way to make that longing go away. It might even lodge it down further, drive it into the core of you, where it hardens and knots up, until it can't be dissolved.

My hurt made my sister's fame seem sinister. Not only because of envy, because of anger, but because of loss. I saw fame changing her life, pulling her away. The more I saw her name in print, her face reproduced, the more I suspected she was always on people's minds when they interacted with me, the more difficult it was to experience her as real, as a soft, warm body. That's not because she was any closer to dead. Nor was it her fault. It's what fame, the massiveness of its distortions, did to me.

In lots of dictionaries the third or fourth entry under "name" is some version of "a famous person." That's the definition I scan to, the one that catches, the one that rings in my ears. A name is always a stand-in, a metonym for a whole person. But fame pulls the being and the name even further part. The name becomes bigger than the being. My proximity to fame made me cynical, and that cynicism made me suspicious that the purpose of a name is simple: we require a stable identity so that we can be known.

I can't write about my name without writing about being known—the desire to be known, the disdain for and the fear of that desire, the sense that people believe they know you before you've even revealed yourself, and, as a result, the desire to hide.

There are parallels between what is disorienting about being known and what is disorienting about being gendered. Both circumscribe who you can or cannot be before you have spoken.

When I returned to LA, after time with my parents, I deleted all my social media. I didn't want to exist outside my body. I didn't want to feel I was in anyone's mind, ever. And I didn't want to see my name anywhere, written out in letters. It made me dizzy. It made me humiliated. It made me feel evil.

The chemicals of the new antidepressant had leveled out, but I still wasn't able to do much. I did walk every day to a flat ridge at the top of a steep dirt path, up the road from Lake's and my house. We call it "the thinking spot." If it hasn't rained for a long time, the ridge is just tan dust, littered with beer cans, shards of glass, and other dispossessed items as wide-ranging as a car hood, a children's bicycle, or a moldy "For Sale" sign. But when it rains, even for a day, grass sprouts up overnight, green blades pricking through mud. There's a rope swing, too, hanging from the low, spindly branch of a black walnut tree that looks like a tarantula.

At the thinking spot, I developed a habit, a hobby even, of collecting and making piles of trash. I organized the shards of glass into colors, like Venus (mother of Grace, the boy), whom I met at the sea glass beach in Northern California. When the piles got big enough, I brought up a garbage bag and filled it up, then slid down the path with what I'd collected and emptied it into nearby waste and recycling bins. The trash collecting calmed me. I liked being around anonymous refuse. I liked cleaning up chaos.

Also at the thinking spot, looking up at the black walnut tree branches quivering against the sky, I began the practice of trying to fill up every single pocket of my body with air, in order to feel myself from the inside out. Into my toes, into the arches of my feet, into my shins. Into my bladder, into my anus, into my hip bones, into my colon, into my ribs, my armpits, and even my breasts.

The more of myself I felt, the more that Grace just...drifted away. As if I'd closed my eyes for a long time and when I opened them she was far out at sea, on the other side of a swell, a white spot appearing and re-appearing in the water. There was no bringing her back, even if I wanted to.

I wanted to be nameless, nothing, the opposite of known. And yet I had no idea how. To aspire to be known was the only way I'd ever been taught to be alive.

The less I wanted a name, the more compulsively I named everything I saw. Tree. Glass. Car. Hill. Gun. Chicken. Knife. Shit. Cunt. Acorn. Caterpillar. Restaurant. I lay in the grass at the thinking spot and imagined myself as every other thing in the universe I could ever name, so diffuse and infinite as to be indiscernible, as to be unnameable.

* * *

In November I told Joshua I didn't want to be called Grace anymore. Each day I imagined myself with the name of a different man I pulled from the folds of my memory. Samuel, the name of my mother's father, an orthodontist who used to let me play with his dentistry tools. He had three last names over the course of his life, each one less Jewish sounding than the last, and told me stories about a talking shark that had followed him "from Coney Island to Saipan."

Simon, the first two syllables of Samuel's original last name. Edward, my late uncle, a lawyer who looked like a more clean-cut version of my father and had an encyclopedic knowledge of Civil War history. Michael, the archangel, and my third-grade teacher, who taught me about white holes, the opposite of black holes, out of which the disappeared matter emerges into another dimension. Mark (Wahlberg). John, the boy from America they found hiding in the caves in Afghanistan after 9/11, whose voice haunted me as Amelia Earhart's had before him. Amelia's voice had been a high-pitched whistle through the sky. John's lips were so chapped, his tongue so dry, that he could barely get words out. I remember seeing pictures of John on the front pages of the papers at the subway newsstands when I was a kid. He was naked, blindfolded, and tied up. Kids at school said mean things about John and protective rage surged up in me. He'd felt so lonely, so isolated, that he'd done something much of the world saw as evil just to be embedded

118

in a community. At least, that's why I imagined he'd done it. They brought him back to America for a trial, to decide whether he would get the death penalty or go to prison forever. At night, when I closed my eyes, I saw his white, bearded skeleton face on the inside of my eyelids, loneliness behind everything. He looked dead even though he wasn't, yet.

I remembered the name one morning, sitting out on the porch in the mist before Joshua or Lake woke up. In the room where Joshua and I slept at my parents' house, there was a piece of green paper, framed and hung on the wall. It was the list of names my mother had chosen from when I was born. Betty, Myrna, Georgia, Esther, Jane, and a dozen more girls' names. Grace was circled. On the right side, under the "Boy" column, just one name. Cyrus.

I whispered it, said it slowly, pressed my tongue against the back of my teeth to whistle the first syllable, pushed my lips out for the soft *r*, let my mouth curl around the *us*. Then I wrote it down, again and again. I wrote a big capital C on a sheet of paper from one of my yellow legal pads. The C opened its mouth for the following letters. Then I practiced in cursive. Then all caps. Then block letters.

Over breakfast, I slid the paper across the table to Joshua, facedown.

"Don't say it out loud," I told them. "I'm too shy to hear it."

They didn't look up, just scribbled, then slid the paper back over to me. They'd written an acrostic, "Grace" and

119

"Cyrus" intersecting at the *r*, an uneven crucifix. I folded the piece of paper up and put it in my jacket pocket. We didn't talk about it anymore. I told no one else.

A couple of days later, Joshua called me Cyrus during sex. I was on top of them, in the dark, their arms wrapped around the back of my neck. It was the kind of sex that made me feel like a man, which we'd been having more of lately. They said the name and I came, without anticipating it.

The next night they said it again. Cyrus. This time, impulsively, I told them to shut up. I squeezed my eyes shut and rolled over onto my back, unmoving. The humiliation of asking to be something you're not. I'd already been denied when I asked to be called Jimmy years ago.

I apologized to Joshua profusely for having been so curt.

The next day I taped the piece of yellow paper to the wall inside my closet, so I'd have to look at it whenever I changed clothes. Sometimes I admired the shapes of the letters; other times I averted my eyes.

Cyrus remained a stranger whose ways I was trying to understand.

How would he wear his hair? How would he cuff his pants? Would he be bold with his opinions or listen and offer insight only when asked for it? Would he stay up late, meeting strangers? Would he take pleasure in spontaneity? Would he know that he was his best self at six a.m., put himself to bed early with his papers and pencils organized geometrically on the desk? Would he have lovers or prefer solitude? Would he push his hair back or let it fall in his face? Would he believe that the way things are can be changed or accept their immutability and go inward? Would he lift weights or would he run when he was moved to, even in the dark, or when it was raining? Would he have countless acquaintances or a handful of friends he kept extremely close? Would he believe in marriage? Would he be on time? Would he have Instagram? Would he be a vegetarian or would he buy steak at the grocery store to cook in a pan when he was home alone? Would he do ketamine on a Saturday night or sit upright at the table, reading, with a pot of herbal tea he'd just brewed? Would he meditate? Would he be a masochist? Would he take long walks with no destination? Would he read novels or philosophy? Would his journal entries be narrative or poetic? Would he travel? If he traveled, would he do it alone? Would he have sex with strangers and tell no one it had happened? Would he have sex with men? Would he be on Grindr? If he was on Grindr, would he post shirtless selfies, or ones of him in button-downs, his hair parted on the side, his glasses still on? Would he keep his cocks on the windowsill, or in a box in a drawer in his closet? Would he ever wear sneakers? Would he ever wear khakis? Would he look gay or straight? Would he be happy living in the country? Would he be polyamorous? Would he be celibate? Would he give a stranger a ride? Would he make money? Would he care about money? Would he be successful? Would he value success? Would he ever give advice? Would he wear short-sleeved polo shirts? Would he keep his word? Would he answer emails immediately? Would he speak another language? Would he be a socialist? Would he have opinions? If he had opinions, would he share them? Would he be a service top, or a dominant top, or a power bottom, or a submissive bottom, or all of the above? Would he have a beard? Would he have hair on his chest? Would he be able to fall in love? Would he rather wake up alone? Would he be a father? Would he have a dog he took with him everywhere? Would the dog be big? Would he cry? Would he introduce himself as Cyrus or Cy? What truth did the name contain? Was Cyrus inside of me already or had I invented him?

I told a few more close friends about Cyrus, mostly in texts or emails. It was too scary to say it out loud. But the name spread. Soon I was running into people who called me "Cy," even though I'd never asked them to. Quickly, it seemed irreversible. I mourned Grace each time I was addressed as Cyrus. The new name rang with guilt for abandoning the old one, as if I'd been tasked with Grace's care and I'd harmed her.

When people asked me what I wanted to be called, I froze. "Either is fine," I'd say, or, "Whichever you prefer."

Being addressed was a constant reminder of my own lack of self-knowledge. I asked Joshua to call me nothing for a while.

When people asked me how I'd picked the name, I was hesitant to admit its place on my parents' green list. My selection of Cyrus suggested loyalty as opposed to differentiation. But seeing "Cyrus" written in my mother's looping script comforted me. As if Cyrus had always been there, waiting in an adjacent dimension.

When I went places where I had to meet new people, I tried to swallow my words while introducing myself. If people asked me my name, I pretended I couldn't hear them. If they asked again, I said whatever came into my mind first. I'd tell one person in a circle I was Cyrus, then turn to another and say I was Grace. Cyrus, Grace, Cyrus, Cy, Grace. I noticed that when I introduced myself as Grace, my voice had a higher pitch. I was more concerned with politeness, adjusting my voice and speech to make whomever I was speaking to more comfortable. Cyrus, on the other hand, felt entitled to speak briefly, or not speak at all.

The two names talked over each other, always on my mind, an etching on the inside of my eyelids, like the letters of the alphabet had been when I first learned to write. Stop signs, billboards, typewritten bulletins. Cyrus and Grace floating over everything, shrinking and growing, switching places between foreground and background. I felt if I didn't choose one, I would cease to be.

I didn't know why I was doing it, stepping into this uncertain identity with no plan. When friends changed their names, it seemed clear that it was a matter of survival. Their birth names had simply stopped being livable. I held myself to different standards: Why wasn't I strong enough to exist inside Grace? Did I hate myself? Did I hate my family? Did I wish to kill my former self and begin anew? Was I so naive as to think that a new name could shepherd me into a new existence, one that hurt less? Did I think a new name would cut the cord between me and my whiteness, my power, my access? I would always be what I'd always been, no matter what I called myself.

Somewhere deep in my unconscious I still believed that not feeling like a woman was a personal failing. Something was wrong with me. No matter how much I read, how many people I talked to, I still believed that if I were whole, I wouldn't have to change myself.

I started having the dream about walking behind my childhood self again. In the dream I held Grace's hand while she led me around. Her small hand fit perfectly inside mine. Other times I lay on my back while she read to me from a picture book and stroked my hair. She was just learning to read. She wobbled through words, asking me the meaning of unfamiliar ones. I walked around with her on my back, arms gripping my neck and legs gripping my waist. I felt like her father.

I didn't want to admit how betrayed I felt by my body, and how angry that betrayal made me. I tried for a long time to banish anger from my emotional vocabulary. I pushed it down until I couldn't even recognize it. It moved to my edges: twitches in my neck, compulsive blinking, the scabs I picked on my scalp, my habit of pulling out large patches of my leg hair. What a delusional thing to feel: that my soul, somehow, ended up in the wrong container. I wasn't entitled to anger.

A Year Without a Name

Joshua visited when they could, and I saw a handful of friends, but everything outside my own amorphousness was foggy and difficult to recall. I relied on routines and repetition to make the days feel bearable. Breathing from the inside out, like I did at the thinking spot. Rearranging the row of objects on my windowsill every day. Filling a vase with water, and nothing else, and counting how many days it took for the liquid to evaporate. Refolding all the clothes in my closet every day and piling them according to different patterns, like texture, color, or shape.

I decided, with more resolve than ever before, not to drink. As painful as it was to be inside myself, I had an uncanny conviction that I needed to feel all the contours of this being. I couldn't float away. I told a friend that I was scared not to take a sip of something when my heart started pounding in my chest. They told me that every time I wanted to dissociate, I should look for the color red and let it fill me up.

As it turned out, red was always there. Lines of red neon light on the highways, drawn out into the valleys. Red bougainvillea petals on Future Street, on Isabel Street, on all the tight alleys in the neighborhood. Piles of dry red bougainvillea dust in the gutters, whipped up by the wind. The red frame around the picture above my bed that Antonia took in 2016 of my torso, cut off below the chest. My red denim jacket. Red antennae lights on the ridge of the San Gabriel Mountains. Red cars, red roofs, red signs. The glow around the sunset on particularly foggy days.

125

Exit signs. Stop signs. The blood under my fingernails when I picked my head. Red reflections on the water. Red on the horizon all the time.

It made me feel safe and calm to keep my room in perfect order. Clothes folded in squares. A shelf of eight shirts, a shelf of eight pairs of pants, and twelve hangers for jackets and button-downs. Every piece of clothing had to have singular meaning and be something I would wear in the span of two weeks; otherwise, I took it to the church thrift shop at the bottom of the hill. A suit jacket that used to be my father's, a worn-in white T-shirt a friend had given me, the striped rugby shirt with the William Blake quote written across the front: "Bring me my bow of burning gold." The next line of the poem is "Bring me my arrows of desire." I told myself it was a lesson in not making other people the center. I wore the shirt so I would have to be alone with myself, to direct the arrows of my desire toward sensations, not people.

I got through my bouts of debilitating anxiety by running up and down the stone staircase near my house until I was so out of breath I couldn't think. If it was late in the afternoon, the sun was a little lower and a little pinker each time I got to the top of the staircase. There was always some change to track at the bottom of my descent, too: a brown caterpillar getting closer to the grape soda can wedged in the dirt on the other side of the railing; a spider hanging off a dead agave plant.

It calmed me down to calibrate my body to the movement,

however big or small, of nonhuman things. The earth was rotating, the caterpillar was inching, and I, a thing, ran, panted, and paused. When I finished the cycle—up five flights and down five flights, five times—I walked slowly back home, almost without thoughts.

It was still warm enough to sit outside on the balcony at night. I wore shorts, no shirt, put my legs up on the railing. If I didn't look down, I could summon the sensation of flatness where my chest was. If I couldn't ignore my breasts, I pushed the extra flesh toward the center, to the sides, down over my ribs. I pretended it was butter, that I was spreading it thin.

In the evenings, music drifted up the hillside from backyard parties at people's houses. The sound filled the neighborhood. Joshua and I slept with my door to the porch open at night, so that we could hear the music, dogs barking, horns from the train tracks by the river. It calmed me down to feel like earth was one big room. If I could hear everything in the room all at once, then I existed as simply a part of it, and I was okay. I wanted every particle to be its own center such that I felt held in the world, no matter where I was.

The objects of my desire seemed smaller and less grandiose than ever before. I fantasized about walking down the hill in my neighborhood in a T-shirt, with a flat chest and nothing binding my breasts, the wind pressing the fabric against my skin. I fantasized about pulling my shirt off from the collar, instead of from the bottom seam, like men in movies did. I fantasized about sleeping on my stomach, without breasts between me and the mattress. I fantasized about driving down the mountain in a convertible, top down, leaning back in the driver's seat, open to the world instead of hunched over in hiding, like the teenage boys in tank tops who lived by the lake where we spent the summer. In the fantasies I was euphoric but calm, not at all lonely even though I was alone.

I saw him in glimpses. When I walked by a mirror and caught sight of shoulders that were broader than hips, a face with a sharp jaw and thick brows. When I saw my hands on the steering wheel of my car, veins swelling as I turned. When I squatted to lift heavy things and bounced back up with ease. In quotidian moments I saw him, someone I admired, even lusted after.

But these moments of alignment made the misalignment that much more unbearable.

7

How do i chronicle a year during which, for the most part, I was waiting? Waiting to correct my aberrated condition. How do I turn waiting, its fits and starts, into a narrative of self-realization?

Much of how I spent the year was managing waiting with control. I measured my food, the perfect ratio of carbs, protein, and lipids. Thirteen grams of fat per meal, thirty-five grams of protein, thirty-five grams of carbs. Often, these stats were met by a giant bowl of oatmeal and Greek yogurt, with no toppings, that I shoveled into my mouth with a spoon until I felt sick. If I couldn't finish it, I put the bowl back in the fridge and returned to it as soon as I had an appetite again. Eating to build muscle mass required force-feeding. I had to eat past fullness, past disgust, swallow down bland bites even though I'd trained myself to think that the more I ate the more I'd look like a woman. But the force-feeding worked, in a way. I couldn't see myself changing, but other people told me I was getting bigger, more angular, standing up taller.

In attempting to change my body, I could impose the possibility of a narrative onto what felt otherwise unnarrativizable. I went to the gym every other day and split my workouts into push-push-pull and pull-pull-push routines. I watched large men pull their entire bodies up and down, relying only on their shoulder, chest, and back muscles, in sets of twelve, each muscle visibly rippling. Watching them maneuver their bodies was the only thing I let make me furious. I could lift my body if I jumped up to the bar. Otherwise, I just hung there, rendered immovable by gravity. All I wanted was to be able to pull myself up, release, and pull again. That, to have a six-pack, and to have no breasts. It was a type of longing I knew only from romance.

When I got home from the gym, I held my iPhone at different angles in order to take selfies on my bed or in the bathroom mirror, looking for a vertical line down my abdomen, two or three horizontal ones. I couldn't tell in real life if the horizontal lines were muscle or just shadows between rolls of skin. I preferred to look at myself in the photos on my iPhone. I hearted my favorite ones so that I could look through them before going to sleep. Dozens of the same pose, examining the slightest differences. Vanity, sure, but also forensic examination. Looking for evidence, compulsively, for proof that I was changing.

I stopped looking at pictures of other people and stopped wanting to have sex, too preoccupied by my own body to be able to focus on someone else's. If I watched porn, it was just to compare my own form to that of the men in the videos.

Soon I became fixated on getting a convertible. I decided it was the only thing that would make me happy. I don't need to expound on how the convertible represents masculinity and virility in American culture, whether for a bachelor having a midlife crisis or a sixteen-year-old boy in search of a hand job. Everyone already knows that. My fixation could have been easily read as overcompensation. But the desire went beyond that: I imagined that a convertible would let me feel unencumbered, open to the outside world, like the boys who sped up the dirt road in tank tops at the house where we spent the summer when I was a kid. The convertible felt like a roomier metonym than a new name.

I kept two tabs open in Safari: one for convertibles; one for before-and-after pictures of "chest masculinizing" double mastectomies on different plastic surgeons' websites. Convertibles and flat chests. The two melted together. Top down. Top surgery. I started spending exorbitant amounts of time on Craigslist browsing convertibles. A Miata in Tujunga. A 2006 Mercedes Benz SLK in Glendale. A 2004

Mustang in Carson. I lay on my back with my laptop on my chest, burning the skin red, doing comparative analyses.

THIS MUSTANG IS GOOD AS NEW AND HOT HOT HOT!!! Cruising with the top down in this convertible will allow turn every drive into a sublime experience, making you feel one with road. 6-Spd SelectShift. DO NOT CONTACT UNLESS FOR REAL!!!

I went to Van Nuys to test-drive a white Toyota Solara. The seller was an extremely thin Polish woman. Stone statues of Jesus filled her front yard. Her children watched us through a slit in the doorway. I drove the car around the block. It was big and clunky. It shook when I accelerated. Another appendage, it was exactly the opposite of what I needed. I hated it.

I test-drove a Honda S2000 in Hawthorne, accelerating in circles around the flat suburban streets. The leather upholstery was dirty; the car was too low to the ground. The seller was an older man. He thought I was a girl and, being a girl, I felt guilty for not wanting to buy his car.

When I test-drove the cars, I said my name was Grace. I didn't want to watch the sellers struggle with confusion that a name, Cyrus, didn't match my "female" body.

I felt angry every time I had to drive somewhere, even the post office or the gas station, in my dad's old gray Camry. It was dull and unwieldy, even dysphoric. If it sounds like

I let a commodity become a proxy for my identity, that's because I did.

Mitsubishi had manufactured a midmarket two-door, five-seat convertible, the Eclipse Spyder. It wasn't fancy or horse-powered enough to be in any of the "top ten hot convertibles" lists in *Men's Journal* and the like, but for me, it looked the part. Streamlined, aerodynamic, with a bubble butt and rounded headlights like the eyes of a frog. Not quite a proxy, but an object of longing. I'd be lying if I said I didn't personify the car as femme.

I messaged a seller with the name of an ancient Greek warrior and she told me to meet her outside a 7-Eleven in East Hollywood. The word "Spyder" was engraved in paint-splash font on the floor mats. The stitching on the leather steering wheel and gearshift looked like the swooping incision lines in the post-op chest masculinization pictures, skin pulled taut at the seam.

Driving in my convertible made me feel joy again. I left the house more, not to see anyone or go anywhere in particular— just to drive around the mountain in the morning before the sun was too bright, or drive the length of the 2 Freeway late at night. I leaned back in my seat, my right hand guiding the steering wheel, my left arm draped out the window. It was a cinematic imitation—a young man drives toward his future—but it made me delight in who I was. When I was in my convertible I was of earth, a part of it, connected to the shared, miraculous impermanence of everything.

It was in my convertible on San Fernando Road, at the stoplight by Cazador Street, that I decided to contact two of the surgeons whose websites I'd kept open as tabs for two months. I wanted to wear a loose shirt in my car, hold my shoulders all the way back, feel the wind against my chest under the fabric. I cried at the relief of granting myself permission. I pressed my forehead against the steering wheel, full of adoration for my Spyder and the permission it—she—had made possible.

Joshua wanted to come with me to San Francisco for my surgical consultations, but I told them I needed to go alone. I couldn't think when I woke up next to them. I just needed to be, without translation. I had no energy for the work of explanation. My own feelings about the surgery were too convoluted for communication, a lust I didn't have words for, yet.

My story isn't resolved enough for me to believe that I have an unquestionable right to my own gender-confirmation surgery. I do *believe* it, in one part of myself. At the very least, because I know I should. Because it's my body, and I have to live in, with, and as it. Let me pilot it.

But it's not that simple for me. My brain monologue sounds like this, spoken in a cacophony, not a linear progression of ideas: My breasts have felt invasive since they started to grow; every time I remember they are there, which is constantly, I am defeated; I have the right to augment my body in order to make it livable; the only reason I need the surgery in the first place is because the tyrannical gender binary has made me believe that my breasts are incompatible with my felt gender; if I was truly transgressive I would be able to tolerate the simultaneity of my breasts and masculinity and see them as co-morbid rather than contradictory; the surgery itself is born from a legacy of mainlining gender-deviant people into having bodies that conform to white, colonial myths of manhood and womanhood; the surgery was developed from a legacy of medical experimentation on the bodies of intersex and gender-nonconforming children; the fact that I can access the surgery is dependent on my ability to perform the mental "capacity" to prove that I am sane enough to get it; those unable to perform "health" are excluded from the very same surgery.

So proceeds my monologue, bolstered by compulsive re-search and information consumption, because I cannot face the immensity of my own longing.

What can I say? I want it. Is wanting enough? I need it. Is needing enough? Perhaps if I levy a strong enough critique, I can argue myself out of wanting and/or needing it.

I went to see Zack, my best and oldest friend alongside Jessica. They live in Riverside, with a spotted cat named Jynx, in a backhouse, on a dirt road, near the base of Mount Rubidoux, which looks like a pile of tan boulders stacked precariously by a giant. Zack and I are the same height, but they're lankier, a long, willowy person. I have always envied the way they dive into water, a slice through the surface, then bounce back up as if they are going to fly away entirely.

We'd called each other "brother" for a while, long before either of us had admitted, or even manifested, that we might have been something other than women. Somehow, the word made what was unknowable about our future seem less scary. They were the only person I'd ever called brother, the only person I'd ever felt that way toward.

That afternoon we walked to the summit of Mount Rubidoux, where a white stone crucifix casts a shadow over the mountain. Sitting on some rocks near the top, Zack told me about a dream they'd had the week before. They didn't want to say the dream out loud because of how much it scared them. I probed. This was part of our dynamic. I like to think that they have taught me to respect the natural pace of emergence, and I have taught them how to put change in motion by speaking. I like to think that, for these reasons and more, we need each other.

Finally they revealed that, in the dream, they had looked in a mirror and seen a man staring back at them. They'd woken up wishing they could unsee him.

"I don't want this," they said.

"I don't want it either," I said.

We walked back down the mountain together, mostly silent.

The following week I drove up to San Francisco with Zack and Jessica for the surgical consultation. The night before the consultation, at a party, I saw someone I thought was hot and decided I would walk up to them and introduce myself, unprompted.

"My name is Cyrus," I said, without faltering.

We left the party and walked around Lake Merritt. We kissed leaning against a railing, next to a drained-out part of the lake caked in goose shit. She was the first person I'd kissed who only knew me as Cyrus. We walked more, toward where she lived. I told a story in which someone addressed me as Grace, without thinking. As soon as the word left my mouth, I tensed up as if I'd been caught in a lie, one in a long line of men going to new cities and conning strangers with new names.

"I'm sorry," I said. "I just changed my name. I'm still getting used to it."

She smiled like it was normal and kissed me on the cheek goodbye.

The next morning I wrote her a message: "Hey, it's Cyrus. Last night was fun."

"I thought your name was Tyrex," she wrote back.

I borrowed a friend's car and drove over the Golden Gate Bridge, stopped to go to the beach at Fort Baker, because that seemed like the kind of thing I ought to do, alone, en route to becoming myself. I took off my socks and my glasses and put them inside one of my boots. I rolled up the legs of my jeans. I stepped ankle-deep into the frigid water, with my coat still on, then lay in the sun breathing into my breasts, scanning for nostalgia, fear of loss, attachment. All the blocks were analytical; historical and political arguments. I couldn't find the sensation of attachment anywhere in my torso, or maybe I had no idea what to look for.

The surgeon's office was in a strip mall medical center in Marin, across the parking lot from an organic grocery store, a pharmacy, a Starbucks. I sat in the waiting room across from a girl who looked maybe fourteen or fifteen, there with her mother. I didn't want to assess her gender, to find proof that she had undergone transformation, but my eyes traveled to the parts of her body that would reveal the truth I was looking for. Her hands, her arms, her neck. This was a gender-confirmation surgeon, after all. Why would a regular fourteen-year-old girl in ballet flats and lip gloss, the kind I would have fantasized about as a teenager, be waiting for an appointment?

The consultation was brief, maybe ten minutes total. The doctor, handsome and charismatic, a chest tattoo peeking over the top of his shirt collar, had me undress from the waist up. I pulled off my shirt, shimmied out of the binder, looked at myself straight on. Breasts hanging there, white lumps, with the miraculous power to pull my attention away from anything and everything else, to hold all the meaning in the entire room, to foreclose all potential.

"Beautiful," the surgeon said, as he traced his finger along the underside of the left one. "I can already see the definition of your pectoral muscle."

"Is that good?" I asked.

"Yes. We'll make the incision along that line. Very good. You're an excellent candidate."

Candidate, as if I'd been selected, as if I might really win. My parents didn't know I was in San Francisco, didn't even know I was seeing a surgeon, but I had an overwhelming urge to call them, to tell them what I'd accomplished.

"Mom," I'd say. "Dad. I'm an excellent candidate."

Back in LA, after the surgical consultation, I befriended Roman. I recognized him from the internet. He'd run an Instagram account where he posted pictures of transmasculine people in diverse settings and iterations of hotness. I looked at the account often to make myself feel less scared of what I worried my future held. I'd been looking at pictures of Roman for two years, watching his jaw square out and his body grow leaner the longer he took testosterone. He'd moved back to Orange County, where he was working construction. I invited him over to our house. We drank tea and ate a chocolate bar—he was sober—and drove in his truck to a party downtown. His truck was full of dirty clothes, fast-food containers, construction equipment, old coffee cups. Outside the party he reached into the back seat for a rumpled wifebeater. He was hungry, so he took a bite of cold scrambled eggs from a discarded takeout container. It made me squeamish, the smell of his car, the indiscretion of his consumption, the unbridled way he lunged out of the vehicle. I studied his every gesture.

As soon as we entered the party he started dancing, hard and fast. He took off his wifebeater and hung it from the back pocket of his boot-cut jeans. He moved like a go-go boy, a lithe Mark Wahlberg. Controlled, but with sway. His biceps and pecs flexed even when he moved imperceptibly. He closed his eyes while he danced, forehead up. He looked like a man, a beautiful young man. A real man, unlike me. I was a girl obsessed with men, their muscles, their expressions, their movements.

My envy made me nauseous and I left the party without telling him.

The next day I called the LGBT Center to make an appointment to procure testosterone. They had no availability. I called another clinic. They were booked too. I called a third and made an appointment for two months out. I didn't give up or back down. Three times I said, "I'd like to make an appointment to begin hormone replacement therapy. I'm assigned female at birth and I'd like to start taking testosterone." No thought, just action.

Roman offered to let me use his testosterone while I waited for my prescription. I drove down to San Pedro to meet him by the Port of Los Angeles. Down the 110 in my convertible, until I could see the cranes above the harbor. We met outside a sandwich shop, on a corner in a quiet neighborhood near the ocean. Suburban ranch houses, American flags. He ordered a french dip sandwich and I ordered one too. He eats whatever he wants, without concern. I followed suit, pretending not to fear any deviation from my dietary regime.

We slid through a chain-link fence and walked down a long, skinny incline to the beach. Round stones and sheets of shelf rock; swirling tide pools. One rock had graffiti on it: "Fuck Love 2018." Another tag, in the same handwriting: "Love Forever." I wanted to find the ruins of the old White Point Hot Spring Hotel, a resort that collapsed in the twenties. I'd read that there were still pieces of the hotel's foundation visible when the tide was low. I loped after Roman, who stepped sturdily from stone to stone. The bottom of my pants got wet. I slipped a few times.

On the way back up from the beach, we passed a group of men drinking beer and watching the sunset. They nodded at us.

"Hey, man," they said. "Hey, man." Men saying hey to men. I didn't talk, lest I break character and ruin the scene.

We drove around San Pedro in my car with the top down. At the base of a hill, I heard flapping, squawking, air parted by feathers. A long shadow passed over us, blocking the remaining sunlight. A peacock landed in the middle of the street, galloped toward an alleyway, its tail billowing behind it. More squawking, then another peacock in the road. Then another, then another. We must have seen a dozen on one street.

I hadn't seen peacocks since Zoya and I had walked by the tree in front of the moon, the day we'd gotten our picture taken. Since then I had associated peacocks with her, with the unrealized potential of our love affair. At one point not so long ago I'd wanted the peacocks to be a sign that Zoya and I would be together. Now a peacock would be the bird I saw the first day I took T. Was I nearing the end of my story?

Roman and I parked at a lookout, the containers of the port stacked on the horizon under fluorescent stadium lighting. He'd prepared a syringe for me with one dose. I lifted my shirt up and he grabbed my stomach flesh in his left hand, wiped it clean with alcohol. I looked out at the cranes and containers. Uncharacteristically, I didn't ask any questions. I didn't ask how he'd do it or what it would feel like when he stuck it in. I didn't look at the packaging, ask where the testosterone came from, research its history, the conditions under which it was made. I just sat there, quiet, let him insert the needle in me and squeeze thick liquid into a pocket of subcutaneous abdominal fat.

I didn't feel anything until he pulled the needle out. The sting of the liquid pooling under my skin, then relief.

We hugged goodbye without exchanging words. I drove home up the 110 with the top still down, even though I was cold. My heartbeat was low and steady. In between my legs, pressure, like something was growing. My brain picked up sensation in parts of my body it hadn't before: eyelids, fingernails, elbows; tongue, hair follicles, shins. The headlights on the highway had weight; the wind had a taste; the clouds hummed. I was of the scene, not outside it looking in. I was. I was. I was. I was. I woke up the next morning, still pulsing.

8

In JUNE, THE SURGEON called to tell me that a slot for a double mastectomy had opened up on July 2. I wasn't supposed to get surgery until October; I'd convinced myself I needed the summer to prepare emotionally and physically for the procedure. To shave off more excess femininity, to stop drinking *entirely,* to finish my book, to abolish my need for validation once and for all. When it came time for surgery, I'd be Cyrus. Settled and secure. Unburdened of Grace's most unpleasant qualities.

But with the prospect there, it seemed unfathomable to wait another five months. What would I do? The same thing I did every single day, for 155 more days? How much more could I learn from waiting? My desire proved to be uncontainable.

I committed to the new surgery date, knowing that my closest friends wouldn't be able to change their schedules with such short notice. I would ask my parents to care for me during my recovery. I had previously told them not to come, for fear that any glimpse of concern or confoundment would preclude my capacity to feel relief. I feared their care, what I might owe them in return.

For many months, my communication with my parents had been primarily shaped by misunderstanding. I couldn't bring myself to tell them what was true: that I was getting the surgery, no matter what; that I'd started hormones; that I had a new name, albeit a name I was still easing into. I couldn't tell whether I was withholding these truths to protect myself from judgment, or because of some deep will toward privacy, even obfuscation. My parents were attached to their second daughter. Disgust rose in me when I imagined being anything else to them, a similar nausea to the one I'd felt when I was young and I thought about them having sex. I was not convinced that I could fit inside the category of child, whatever the gender. Child, the sweetest property of all.

The new surgery date triggered action. I wrote them a short, succinct letter: "I am trans," I wrote. "Not intellectually, or partially, or aesthetically. Fully, deeply, transgender."

Despite my belief that anyone, irrespective of how they do or do not augment their body, is free to disidentify with the gender they were assigned at birth, I deferred to simplicity.

"We understand," my father wrote back. "Thank you."

"Good morning, sunshine," my mother texted me. "Or should I say good morning, son-shine."

My confession of utter transness sacrificed nuance for legibility. I defaulted to the trope that I was born in the wrong body. That I had the soul of a man. Which implied that I believed in such a thing as a man in the first place. Which implied that I believed that, were I to live as a man, I would finally be okay.

But I didn't have time to be rigorous. I just needed them to believe me. At least, enough for me to believe myself.

The week before the surgery, I got a letter from my insurance provider:

A request has been made for coverage of "top" surgery to help with your change from female to male gender. We are unable to approve at this time. We require that you must have a desire to live and be accepted as a member of opposite sex for at least six months. The letter from your therapist indicates only "recent months." Therefor [sic], you don't meet our requirements that you desire to live and be accepted as male for at least six month [sic].

The name of the physician who wrote the rejection letter was Jim. Dr. Jim. In his capacity as assessor of my surgery

145

application's merits, Dr. Jim utilized circular logic so effectively that he almost convinced me. He was right, after all: I had not unilaterally desired to be a male for more than six months. At most, I could desire it for a minute at a time, maybe two.

My parents volunteered to cover the surgery up front so long as I contested the denied claim and reimbursed them after the fact. (If they paid for the removal of my breasts, would I think of them every time I felt my new chest? Would I remain theirs?) I accepted their money. Of course I accepted their money.

My father woke me up the morning of the procedure at eight. I washed my face and chose an outfit: a button-front shirt, to put on when I woke up after the procedure, loose athletic pants, slip-on loafers. I went into the kitchen of the suburban home we'd Airbnb'd, where my father waited for me. We were wearing virtually the same outfit.

"Morning, girlie," he said.

Feeling too indebted to correct him, I breathed in, shut my eyes briefly, tried to hold on to the notion that Cyrus was more than a myth I'd summoned into existence.

We sat in the kitchen for a while, reading the paper. My mother came downstairs, then my sister. She'd come up for my surgery, even though her life was hectic and full of sadness. It comforted me that she was there, though I didn't tell her.

We all got into my parents' rental car to drive the eight minutes to the surgical center. My father drove and it was like every other time the four of us had shared a car, except I sat in the front passenger seat instead of my mother. I turned on the radio. I looked out the window. I hoped the ride wouldn't end. I thought about asking him to turn around. I wondered if it was too late. I wasn't wearing a binder, either—the first time, I think, in five years that I'd ridden in a car somewhere new, unbound. I reached my hands under my shirt and squeezed my breasts. Was I supposed to have more of a ritual than this?

My father asked me how I was feeling.

"Good," I said. I heard myself talking, but my ears were ringing.

No matter how many people reassured me by describing their own experience of surgery, I couldn't shake the fear that I wouldn't wake up. Just something about time collapsing like that: conscious one second, unconscious the next, the space between disappeared, a long-awaited shift occurring in darkness. My mother comforted me by describing the calm before anesthesia: wrapped in warm blankets, the fentanyl hitting your system and relieving all worry, the sounds of nurses and doctors preparing themselves around you. "You'll feel so good," she said. "I'm jealous."

They laid me down on a crucifix-shaped table in the surgery room: arms outstretched, legs spread. My friend had warned me it would feel sacrificial. I scanned the room for red as they started to pump fentanyl through the IV— red was something to ground and center me, pull me into continuity. But everything was white, pale blues, yellow, gray plastic. I lifted my head. The doctor saw me searching and asked what was wrong. I was about to say, "Can you get me something red?" when I saw, in the lower right-hand corner of my view, five letters—F-O-C-U-S—in bright red font, across the bottom of the door.

"Why's it say that?" I asked the nurse.

"So we focus," she said. My spine got warm; I liquefied.

I awoke to someone saying "Cyrus."

"You're in Recovery, Cyrus. You did great. You're all done."

I was shivering a little, already felt tears leaking from my eyes. I knew Cyrus was me, intellectually, but I needed some other aspect to be summoned in order to fully wake up.

"Can you call me Grace?" I said.

"Cyrus" was the name in quotes on my fluorescent green hospital bracelet, but Grace was there, too. She'd been right under the surface today. Horizontal, vulnerable, wrapped up tight. I needed her to be addressed directly in order to move forward.

"You're in Recovery, Grace." I smiled and cried, asked where my parents were. My voice sounded soft, higher, a voice I knew from a long time ago, waking up groggy in the morning to my mother's knock on the door.

"Five more minutes, Momma," the voice said.

The following week passed in a Vicodin-infused haze. I had to wear a hard white compression vest, shaped like a tube top, stuffed with gauze, cotton, and rivets to keep my grafted-on nipples in place. The top kept my chest tight so there wasn't room for liquid to gather and swell me up. When the painkillers started to wear off, I ached at the wound sites, two horizontal incisions at the bottom of my pectoral muscles, where the breast tissue was removed. As part of the procedure, they removed my nipples, resized them, and reattached them in a more masculine position; the spot where my nipples had once been tingled and burned. I kept picturing my nipples during the surgery, temporarily placed on the operating table like stickers.

We spent the week in a Cape Cod–style suburban home. There was a white picket fence around the house. Inside, a full bar, a mahjong table, and framed color photos of white couples in pastel clothing standing next to vintage American cars. My parents slept in the master bedroom, which had white carpet, white curtains, white sheets, and two white bedside tables. I stayed in the child's bedroom, in a twin bed with monogrammed pillows. My sister slept in the room next to mine. In the living room, there was a coffee table book called *A Privileged Life: Celebrating WASP Style*. I lay on the sofa under a blanket, unable to get up without my father's help. I flipped through the book's high-gloss pictures. White man after white man after white man, dressed in pastels, beaming. I feared the book was there for a reason, evidence of my worst fears about what this process of so-called masculinization would turn me into. Even in the aftermath of the surgery, my relief was crosshatched by the paranoia that I wanted to be a man

149

because it was easier and because I was awful. How did I know it wasn't my fault, my shortcoming, that I couldn't make the other way—womanhood—work?

I had shaved my head the month before surgery, a close buzz I got at a barbershop, exhausted one day by how consistently I'd been gendered as female with hair down to my shoulders. The haircut was working, insofar as that shallow, cosmetic alteration ensured that I was referred to as "sir" at least half the time.

During my Vicodin naps, I kept seeing Amelia Earhart, John the terrorist, and Joan of Arc swimming through my dream space. Joan's breasts were pulled taut with white fabric, underneath her armor. In one vision, I saw her breasts sliced off in a single sword cut. "Okay, Joan," a man said, "we'll make you who you want to be." She would be flat, two perfect red circles, like the blood moon, where the breasts had been.

A few weeks before surgery I asked a writer I admired how they know when a book is finished. They responded with a question: "When did you believe your name was Cyrus?"

The answer was never, or sometimes, or not yet, fully. Conviction comes in bursts, as does fraudulence. Sometimes I say "Cyrus" out loud and there's an electric click inside me, the click of alignment. The name Cyrus doesn't knock me out of my body. But Cyrus is also tentative, a liberating gesture that I always fear will be taken from me when I'm yanked back to reality by the "truth." That I'm a girl, and a daughter, and to claim anything else is to lie. That I'm consigned to being a liar forever. Who would ever believe me?

The week before my surgery, one of my best friends, Chaya, sent me an email with no subject line quoting a Bible passage on the Tower of Babel, which earth's people built after traveling east to escape a great deluge:

> *Come, let us build ourselves a city, with a tower that reaches to the heavens, so that we may make a name for ourselves; otherwise we will be scattered over the face of the whole earth. Genesis 11: 4.*

The people wished to be known by God, to reach up to the heavens and become stars. God did not approve of this hunger for ascendance, for recognition. And so he destroyed the tower, scrambled its inhabitants across the world. Prior to this, all of earth's people spoke a single common language; from then on, they spoke mutually unintelligible languages. This dispersal was called the confusion of tongues.

God's destruction of the tower implies that the will to "make a name" for oneself is full of ego, deserving of punishment. And some people still believe this: that the will to rename oneself is naive at best, grandiose at worst. That naming oneself is akin to playing God.

But what is the alternative? To let other people play God? To accept the constraints of a given name, as if acceptance is always humble?

If I am a tower, then I name myself with the knowledge that I will be dispersed, not that I will cohere. Any name can be destroyed, can destroy itself. My value is not in my permanence but in the resilience with which I recover, and re-recover, and re-form after the deluge. I know myself only insofar as I know that I will always surprise myself, that "I" will collapse and be scrambled whenever I think my own structure is sound. I know myself only insofar as I know I am not singular, that what I am in this moment is born out of everyone I have known, that when the deluge comes I will be washed away, nameless.

Cyrus is a sign and he may not last. And still, I choose to be him now. I need to be him now. I choose to move toward something like manhood—a mercurial concept in which my belief flickers—because, for reasons I still do not know, it makes me feel closer to earth, to everyone and everything else in the flood.

Seven days after the procedure, a nurse removed the gauze in the doctor's office. She gave me a small hand mirror so that I could look at the contours of my new chest as she peeled away the cotton and removed the stitches from my grafted-on nipples. The left side of my chest was fluttering, like a hummingbird. It looked alive. Along the line of the incision, where the skin buckled together from being restitched, I was pulsing and rippling. It hadn't occurred to me I'd be able to see my own heartbeat. I was right there.

Lake and Roman had driven up from LA to get me. The two of them are in love now. Lake held my right hand and Roman held my left foot while the nurse undressed my wounds. Lake told me later that my eyes rolled back in my head when they took the gauze off. She said I looked like I'd just been beamed down into my body for the first time. It was so disarming for her to watch me be born that she fainted. I saw her register my awe, my fear, then watched her body sway and fall. Roman leaped to the ground and held her head in his hands. I looked from Lake to my nipples, to Roman's hands, to Lake, to my nipples. We were in a triangle, in that moment; it seemed like we all had one head, one heart.

My nipples were gray, almost green in parts. They'd been puckered and pink like raspberries before; the precious nipples my mother and father made. Sweet, soft, graceful nipples. I'd cut them off and tried to get an insurance company to pay for them to be sewed back on. Now I had saucers of dead skin, colors a body only produces when it's struggling to heal.

After the nurse finished taking out the stitches, I stood up and looked in the mirror. I was so much smaller than I'd expected, especially from the side; two or three inches thick, spine to sternum. It seemed impossible that my heart and lungs could fit in there.

I couldn't talk. I went to the bathroom, bent over the sink, let out convulsing sobs. My shoulders were hunched and rounded from the postsurgery compression top I'd had to wear for the last week. My chest was concave; my back was curled. I wept and wept, couldn't stop. I walked through the waiting room, still weeping, past two teenage trans girls with their mothers, out into the medical complex parking lot.

I sat in the back seat as we left the bay and drove down the I-5. We got out to use the bathroom a half hour south of San Jose. It was already over a hundred degrees. I was still hunched over in the button-down I'd worn to the doctor's office. One of Roman's wifebeaters was crumpled on the floor of the car.

"You wanna wear this?"

I unbuttoned the shirt slowly, then pulled the tank top over me without lifting my elbows above my shoulders. I went into the women's restroom and an older woman screamed.

"I'm sorry," I said. "Are you okay?"

When I came back out and told Roman, he said, "You can't use the women's restroom anymore, man."

I walked in circles around the gas pumps while Lake and Roman kissed outside the convenience store. With each circle around the pumps, I tried to push my shoulders back a little farther, chest forward a little more. I tried to uncurl. I was afraid to look down and see my heartbeat twitching again. But each spin around I saw myself in the mirrored windows of the convenience store, tall and skinny, wide shouldered, hunched but trying to stand up tall.

We got home at nine and I attempted to shower. It took an hour, working up the courage to stand in front of the water. I let the water hit the back of my neck and shoulders, wash over my chest from behind so it didn't hit my nipples directly and dislodge the skin grafts. I threw up when I had to take the cotton off my nipples and see the rawness of these pieces of skin trying to reattach to my body. I got nauseous each time I looked down and saw my heart twitching. Why couldn't I look at my own heart?

Finally, dried off, I climbed into bed, turned the lights off, lay on my back. I scanned my whole body for feeling, feet to head, listened to the sounds outside. I laid my right hand over the left side of my chest to keep my heart safe, beating in my palm. I dreamed in the middle of the night that I woke up and a red hummingbird had pushed her way, beak first, through the sutures. I lay on my back and watched her buzz around my room in the predawn light. I stood up and walked over to the screen door, opened it, and watched the hummingbird slip out, down, and over the hillside.

AFTERWORD

SEPTEMBER 12, 2018, was the day my dad started calling me Cyrus. He'd known about the name for five months, but he hadn't been able to make the shape with his tongue and lips. I saw him try, a few times, but he faltered.

When I flew to visit them on September 10, it was the first time I'd been home in nine months. They greeted me as Grace at the door. That night, before bed, he said quietly, "I'm going to say Grace until the last possible moment. Until you tell me I have to stop saying it."

The next day he came with me to a barbershop and sat on a bench behind me while the barber tightened up my crew cut.

"How old are you, son?" the barber asked.

"Twenty-six."

"Oh," he said. "You look young."

I sensed my father, who was sitting behind me, prickle with protectiveness. He stood up, walked over.

"Cy," he said, "I'm going to the car to get my book." He said it with conviction, as if he'd waited to make the proclamation until he was certain he could.

It's been almost five months since my surgery. The incisions on my chest are closed up, except for an inflamed red patch underneath my right nipple that's twice as thick as the rest of the scar. The left side of the scar reaches two inches farther toward my back than the right side. I'm working to be at peace with the asymmetry, even though I don't think it's beautiful. There are hard knots under the surface of the scar that crunch when I press on them. I squeeze them between the side of my pointer finger and the pad of my thumb to break them up. Every two days I peel off strips of beige silicone scar tape and rub vitamin E oil into the tissue. I still can't lift my elbows above my shoulders. I have no sensation in my new nipples, but I have phantom sensitivity toward the middle of my chest, where the nerve endings of my old ones are.

I've been on testosterone for seven months. I give myself the shot on Tuesdays, alternating between the left and right sides of my stomach. The most painful part is the first second, when the needle breaks the skin; after that, it slides in without resistance. I look forward to Tuesdays all week and visualize the needle 90 percent submerged in my abdominal fat when I'm overwhelmed or can't fall asleep. The image calms me down. On Tuesdays, I wait to give myself the shot until I have a moment spacious enough for a proper ritual. Once the clear liquid has dripped into the syringe, I point the needle toward the sky and flick the plastic until the tiny bubbles gather into one pocket of air. I tilt the syringe slightly, back and forth, until it's perfectly level and I can catch the bubble at the needle's entrance. Then I release the remaining air. That's my second-favorite part, other than looking at the needle when it's inside me. The hours after the shot are my most deeply felt hours in the week. My skin tingles and everything looks beautiful. I am close to earth, attuned to and entangled in interconnectedness.

My clitoris is four times as big as it used to be. My skin is oilier. When I'm at the gym, studying men's bodies, I feel a heat in between my legs I've never felt before. Sometimes my eyes involuntarily travel to their groins, and I picture them seated, with their arms behind their head. I'm kneeling in front of them, blowing them.

I have two patches of dark hair where my chin meets my neck. I shave every two or three days, and I touch the stubble all the time when I'm thinking or talking. I was ashamed of the hair at first, as though my masculinity was erupting out of me. But I also fantasize about having more, above my lips, on my thighs, in a triangle over my sternum.

I've tipped over the edge somehow, and now most people in public think I'm a man, or at the very least, a boy. I pitch my voice down at gas stations and convenience stores so as not to confuse anyone I interact with.

People don't talk to me in public the way they used to, on airplanes, buses, or trains, waiting in line for something. Like I am no longer open for dialogue. When I am friendly, I often sense strangers' discomfort, as if I'd only be kind in order to *get* something. To manipulate or accrue more power. I want to say, "But I'm a girl." Or, "I was born a girl." Or, "I was a girl once."

But, of course, I never say that. And, also, I'm not sure if I ever was. Instead I just pitch my voice back up, rupture my masculinity on the off chance that a stranger will understand.

I used to stay home just to avoid the possibility of getting called "she" in public. But sometimes it feels as bad to be a man, especially when women flash their hatred at me. Occasionally, I attempt to use the women's room; I imagine the familiarity will be comforting. But usually, within seconds, a woman chastises me. It's worse when she looks terrified. I feel defeated and horrific, like I've disappointed every single mother I ever wanted to make proud.

It's scarier, if less resonant, when men flash their hatred at me. I was walking down Hyperion Boulevard in Silver Lake the other day, and I saw a tall blond man in a dress shirt approaching from up the block, holding a giant street sweeper across his shoulders.

"You're on the wrong side of the sidewalk, mate," he said. He was British.

"Excuse me?" I said politely, trying to understand.

His eyes got wide. Red and seething. As if upon hearing my voice, he realized something he hadn't yet. He said, "So you're fucking with me, faggot?"

Then he ran at me and swung the street sweeper at my head.

I took off down the middle of Hyperion Boulevard, in my mesh athletic shorts and tank top. As I dodged cars, I thought about how boys made fun of me for running like a girl when I was a girl. How I probably still ran like a girl. But I wasn't a girl anymore: the man with a broom was chasing another man, a feminine man. The anger is never because someone thinks I'm a girl pretending to be a boy. It's because someone thinks I am a man failing to be a man. This type of violence is new to me.

When I don't open my mouth, I can slip into anonymity. Another white boy with his head down. I'm unmarked, invisible, and I like it.

GD is the person I'm in love with now. I call them GD as a joke; those are the initials of a philosopher they used to pretend to like to impress men. They call me GD, too, the initials of my "dead name." I gave them permission. They call me Cyrus when they're talking about me to other people. When we're alone, they call me Jimmy, the chosen name of my childhood that no one acknowledged. I have many names for them, too. Different feelings demand different names.

I spoke to GD every day of my surgery recovery, lying on my back on the twin bed in the child's bedroom. But I omitted GD from my initial narration of that week, which is the last chapter of this book. When I sent them the writing from that week, they asked if I'd left them out because I was ashamed to have fallen in love again, if I thought falling in love signaled a failure to self-actualize.

I told them I wanted to protect them from becoming a character. I didn't like how writing about people made me see them—the moments I'd chosen to write became realer than the moments I hadn't. Sometimes it seems safer to omit, as a form of protection.

But some part of me also hoped, even believed, that if I changed my name, started hormones, and removed my breasts, my need for acknowledgment would lessen. I've read enough Bildungsromans to want an ending marked by personal sovereignty. And I thought I'd get it, at times: independence, autonomy, resolution. Individuation pulls at me even when I think I'm outrunning it.

I had always imagined that I'd be alone after top surgery; single, but still surrounded by friends, family, former partners who have become family. As if, breastless and complete, I would be cured of codependent attachment.

Even though GD and I spoke throughout that week— and, in fact, I was in a near constant dialogue with my closest friends, with former partners, too—I do remember those seven days as if I was entirely by myself. I recall lying on my back in the dark, still but not sleeping, alone in the room of my mind. Under the monogrammed yellow sheets of another family's female child.

It seems contradictory that I could have felt so entirely alone when, as the pages of this book evidence, it is impossible to know myself outside of other people. For so long, I could only catch flares of something that felt like my "self" in the eyes of whomever I desired. Whenever I stopped catching those flares, I chased new sets of eyes.

The truth is that, after all this, I still feel a special kind of euphoria in being witnessed. Something crystalline and hyperreal. Call this being: being in love, or being *with*. This story cannot end with solitary self-reliance. I am more at home in my body than ever before. But there are moments of profound and eternal-feeling aloneness. And still, I seek to be seen.

GD came to Los Angeles ten days after my surgery. I drove to pick them up at LAX in my convertible even though I wasn't supposed to drive yet. I put the shoulder belt behind my back so it wouldn't rub my wounds and I kept my elbows in my lap while I steered. I drove GD to International Road and parked on the other side of a chain-link fence from the airplanes. The top of my convertible was down and they pulled my shirt off over my head. They pressed their ear against my chest to listen to my heartbeat. After, we looked at each other for a long time and they told me my pupils were dilated. They'd been dilated since surgery. They stayed dilated for many weeks after.

Each day GD was in Los Angeles they painted bacitracin onto my nipples with a Q-tip, careful to cover the entire surface with clear ointment. They took pictures on their iPhone every day to document the changing colors: green-gray, purple, yellow, orange, and red.

Later in the summer I went to visit them in Detroit, where they stay in a house on a canal. Their outdoor sink is overgrown with purple morning glory weeds, like the ones in my first memory, that bloom purple for the first part of the day and wrap their vines around the soap bottles or forks we leave on the shelf overnight.

We went to a tributary of Lake Michigan called Torch Lake and I swam for the first time with my flat chest. It was raining and the water was turquoise. There were waves even though it wasn't the ocean. I stood at the shore in my blue underwear, shivering. GD ran ahead and dove into the break. They went way out, farther than I did. I yelled at them to come back. They swam up to me and said I looked like a big boy. "A big boy next to a big lake."

I counted to eight and made myself jump in. The water was cold; it cut across the skin over my heart. I paddled over to GD, trying to swim even though I couldn't extend my arms. I stretched out onto my back and GD held me up, just below the surface. I watched the blue water slosh over my chest. I felt my pupils dilate. I knew GD was watching me stare at my own chest.

Back in Detroit, GD and I went on boat rides in the evening, after they got home from work. One night a neighbor of GD's, a woman drinking a Miller High Life on her sailboat, pointed at me from afar and said, "Who's he?"

GD uses "he" for me. I am appalled by how much I love it. The pleasure is such that it must be a dream I'll wake up from.

He's learning to drive a stick shift. He's never been to the Great Lakes before. He lives in California. He picked me up from work today. I've been making him eat a hamburger a day. He. He. He. He. The more banal the sentence, the deeper the effect.

The more they use "he," the more willing I am to submit to them. I lie on my back, spread my legs, and let them have sex with me the way I would have had sex if I'd let a boy take my virginity. I wear lingerie sometimes. Occasionally, when we have sex, I tell them to call me Grace.

ACKNOWLEDGMENTS

First and foremost, I want to thank everyone—friends, family, partners, partners turned friends turned family— who consented to appearing, in some form or another, in the pages of this book. I am a young writer and I am still learning about the sacrifices we make when we attempt to translate our experience into language. All of you gave me permission to try, with the knowledge that this book, my first, could never render you in your fullness. I am grateful for the patience and the trust. Above all, I am grateful for the conversations—sometimes painful, but always transformative—that took place throughout this process. Writing through life is necessarily a collaboration, and I know that even more deeply than I did when I started this book.

Thank you to the friends who have supported and inspired me over the past two years, as I moved through writing and the previously unthinkable changes that accompanied it: Shay, my first angel, thanks for holding me in your golden glove early on, before I saw all this on the horizon. Doreen and Alex, thanks for the beautiful meals in your beautiful home that have punctuated the last few years; you both inspire me, together and apart. Hazel, art is much less scary when I get to make it alongside you, and time spent with you is art in and of itself. Liv, thanks for being my best bedmate when I needed it. Palma, something tectonic has us drifting closer and closer toward each other.

Rhiya, thank you for the unexpectedly fast friendship. David, let's be each other's foils until the end. Emily S., thanks for being & seeing magenta with me. Geo, I've been made wiser by the expansiveness of your outlook.

Carolyn, thank you for a closeness built over correspondence; in particular, thank you for unteaching me potential; it freed me up to be less afraid of failing. Matt, thanks for telling me to stand behind my work, for pragmatic reassurance. Lex, thank you for writing alongside and motivating me, even with one and a half continents and an ocean between us.

Tourmaline, thank you for inviting me not to lie, with such patience and love. Blaine, thanks for coaxing me to Los Angeles, to a life with more space and plasticity. Amelia, thank god you came here too, and thank god I heard your songs when I did. Lessa, I'm so glad that you realized you were already in the club. Carson, thanks for your magical mind and the best panna cotta in California.

anise, thank you for the poem, even though it was stolen; I'm learning to let language leave when it wants to. Jade, thank you for the grain of red rice, the purple fish, the green beetle; thank you for all the spells. Cassils, thank you for teaching me how to be in my body, after twenty-five years of being elsewhere.

Hannah, what we have continues to push me and then, somehow, to protect me. I'm still riveted. Skye, thanks for waking me up; you made writing seem worth doing and I'm still feeling the ripples of that. And Aviva, patron saint of the naughty and the nice, this book and my world are ripe with symbols you gifted me.

Thank you to Al, Margie, and the orange and blue house on the hill (and the black walnut and guava trees, the red-tailed hawks, the mangy coyotes in the canyon) for giving me the first place that ever really felt like home. Al, you let me grow up and calm down. Sam, so glad you joined us. And, Elias: thank you for teaching me to release instead of resist. Hayden, it's your home too. Thank you for giving me angels and the credence to receive them. You've been a portal.

An immense and inexhaustible thank-you to everyone in CCWP-LA, especially everyone surviving and organizing inside CIW, for giving me a political and spiritual home in Southern California, for making me understand what it means to stay and believe and try. Working alongside and learning from all of you has been an unimaginable honor.

Willa, thank you for pushing me off the cliff, then and now, for what I expect to be a lifetime of mutual cliff pushing. You changed everything.

Alok, your thinking has shaped my work these past few

years, as well as the way I understand the world. Your loyalty has shaped me too. By the end of this project, I'd somehow grown to cherish your incredibly unenthusiastic Google doc suggestions.

Lynne, thank you for your uncanny copyedits, your generosity of wisdom, and the new, right beginning.

Bobbi, I'm grateful for every version you've been thus far and every version you'll be. Thanks for getting me to stick my fingers in the dirt and my toes in cold water. You make infinite births and deaths seem beautiful.

Jerry and Ro, the first writers in my life, thank you for always respecting me enough to give me the adult version of things. Aunt Bonnie and Aunt Susan, I'm so lucky to have your love and your laughter.

Laurie, Tip, and Lee, the fates threw us together in this configuration called a "family." I opt in—not out of obligation, but because I want to do the work. Laurie, I can never tell if you have the soul of a one-day-old baby or a hundred-million-year-old sorceress. Tip, your willingness to relearn and be retaught is remarkable. Laurie and Tip together, thank you for wanting to know me. You could have stayed attached to an idea and you didn't. Lee, we're made of the same material, and when we're able to meet it's the opposite of loneliness. Thank you for continuing to try with me. And thank you to the three of you for always telling me to write, to keep writing, no matter what.

Mary and Danielle, you're family, too. Thank you for everything you do, for all of us.

Acknowledgments

Paul...I can't say I expected you. But here you are, and it makes sense.

Rosie, thank you for showing me the way to honesty, in writing and in life, for accepting that it's a work in progress. Thank you for your Neptune, for the ditch, for suns, and sons, and sonnets.

Em, twenty years of friendship and counting. Thank you for being my coach and my soccer mom, my CEO and my executive assistant, my *Lebensgefährte*. Zan, you're my only brother. My brilliant, beautiful brother. Boozer and Brother, together, my constants. And thank you, of course, to Birdie and Jynx, for taking care of B&B when they needed it most.

Thank you to the whole team at Little, Brown, for the guidance and the support, which cut through my doubt.

Finally, I want to thank Bill and Jean. Bill, you believed in this project at its nascency, told me it was legitimate, even valuable, to write through not knowing. Jean, thank you for being a nurturing friend and a harsh editor, somehow simultaneously. I didn't previously know the two went together. You finally got me to accept that I love writing, that I may, after all, be a writer.

171

ABOUT THE AUTHOR

Cyrus Grace Dunham is a writer and organizer living in
Los Angeles. This is their first book.